P9-AQV-979

Woodbourne Library
Washington-Centerville Public Library
Centerville, Ohio

DISCARD

NO

ALSO BY JIM CAMP

Start with No

NO

The Only Negotiating System You Need
for Work and Home

JIM CAMP

CROWN
BUSINESS
NEW YORK

Copyright © 2007 by James R. Camp

All rights reserved.

Published in the United States by Crown Business, an imprint of
the Crown Publishing Group, a division of Random House, Inc., New York.

www.crownpublishing.com

Crown Business is a trademark and the Rising Sun colophon
is a registered trademark of Random House, Inc.

Library of Congress Cataloging-in-Publication Data
Camp, Jim.
No : the only negotiating system you need for work and home / Jim Camp.
Includes index.
1. Negotiation in business.   2. Interpersonal relations.   3. Persuasion
(Psychology).   4. Problem Solving.   I. Title.
HD58.6.C357 2007
658.4'052—dc22   2007001346

ISBN 978-0-307-34574-5

Printed in the United States of America

Design by Lenny Henderson

10 9 8 7 6 5 4 3 2 1

First Edition

To my children,
Jim and Cynthia, Scott and Meredith,
Todd, Brian, and Kristi

Contents

CONTENTS

CONTENTS

NO

Introduction

The Best Word in the English Language

The best word in the English language must be "yes." You please the other person. You satisfy the request. You get something done; you make a deal. Everyone is happy, break out the bubbly. Likewise, the worst word must be "no." It rubs everyone the wrong way. It implies rejection and intransigence. It stops this deal right in its tracks. It's a killer.

Or so everyone in this compromise- and assumption-based world seems to believe. In truth, this thinking should be flipped on its head. In negotiation, "yes" is the *worst* word. It just betrays a fear of failure and a fear of losing this deal, and it primes you to please the other side, to rush ahead, to compromise early and often, to come to a deal, any deal. "No" is the *best* word. It's what you want to be prepared to say *and to hear.* "No" will liberate and protect you.

Consider Bill, a successful sales rep for Midwest Widgets (a ficticious name clearly, as are all other names in this book), who handles the Dumont account. Midwest has enjoyed Dumont's business for seven years, and there's been no indication that the situation is about to change. Midwest makes an excellent widget and gets a fair price for it. Suddenly, though, the largely ceremonial sales call to Dumont takes a nasty turn. Steve, the new purchasing agent, tells Bill out of the blue, "I'm sorry, but we're changing our widget supplier. I'm fed up with your company's arrogant behavior and have decided to choose from three of your competitors who've been beating down our door for years to get a piece of the action."

Bill, like many salespeople, immediately assumes that Steve
and Dumont are actually maneuvering for a price discount, and
he believes (assumes) his only recourse is to immediately give
in and compromise. Drop the price and save the business. Bill
instantly runs the numbers. How small a discount can he put
on the table and keep the Dumont contract? How large a discount would cost him his job? Almost instinctively, he asks
Steve what price will be required to keep the account. Steve
has to work hard not to gloat in triumph. This was so easy. He
already has Bill exactly where he wants him, and he replies,
"Well, Bill, I appreciate your willingness to give us a better deal,
but I'm not sure you can keep the business at any price. But
I'm willing to go to bat for you with my committee if you
knock fourteen cents off the unit price."

Lose the Dumont account! Bill might as well get out his résumé and put his house on the market. Emotional *chaos* is not
too strong a description of his plight at this moment. His emotions are raging and his heart is pounding, but he is able to
muster the wherewithal to ask for a time-out, which Steve
grants. Bill calls Susan, his sales director. It's a new world with
Dumont, he tells Susan. The only way to keep the account is
with a big discount—fourteen cents per widget. Otherwise,
Dumont is going elsewhere.

Now Susan is a partner in the chaos. Bill's failure would be
her failure. Just as Bill has taken everything Steve with Dumont
has said at face value, she takes everything Bill has reported at
face value. "Do you think he'll take twelve cents, Bill?" Both assume that the fourteen cents is Steve's high number, but he'll
knock it down a little. Neither Bill nor Susan has any idea
what's really going on with Dumont. All they know is that it's a
win-win world: You ask, I give, it's a deal!

I call this compromise- and fear-based negotiation. Steve with
Dumont is playing on Bill and Susan's fear of failure—their fear
of losing the deal. He is rather crudely trying to manipulate

their instinct to say yes and their fear of saying no. This is the oldest game in the book, but it works a million times a day. Meanwhile, I teach and preach the system based on "no," which in a negotiation simply means maintaining the status quo. If Steve wants fourteen cents knocked off the price of each widget, a "no" from Bill just holds things in a safe place. From here Bill can then make a decision whether to give all, part, or none of the increase based on the facts, not the emotion of the moment as he sees his job and possibly his career unraveling.

The impulse to say yes (as advocated in *Getting to Yes,* as well as its many other compromise-, assumption-, fear-, and emotion-based imitators) undermines you, at the very least, while the "no" strategy will liberate and protect you by releasing the emotional pressure in a negotiation. It provides a safe framework within which to determine the best course.

To see how, in brief, let's rewind Bill's story. If Bill is using the "No" system, Steve's bombshell about the fourteen-cent discount doesn't faze him in the least because he responds systematically rather than emotionally. As Bill carefully considers Midwest's mission and purpose, he notes that it's unlikely the company's management will support a significant compromise just because someone asks for it. Judging Midwest by its own standards, Bill decides that Steve and Dumont will have to do better than that.

Bill will ask Steve several questions, all aimed at building Steve's *vision* of what it would mean to Dumont to change its widget supplier. Where have we fallen short, Steve? How many failures has Dumont encountered with the Midwest widget on its production line? How much risk of failure can Dumont absorb with a new, unproven widget? Bill would ask these questions in a certain way, and he would listen to the answers and take notes in a certain way. Of course, he would already know the real answers: the Midwest failure rate, how much risk Dumont can take, and the quality and the price of the competitors' widgets.

In short, Bill will say no to offering a big price discount while giving the negotiation a solid foundation on which to build. So many people in business are afraid that saying no in this way will make Steve walk away, but he won't, believe me. After all, Midwest hasn't been Dumont's widget supplier for seven years for no good reason. In the end, Bill and Midwest may give some ground on price—or they may not. Regardless, that decision would be based on solid information, not assumptions or emotions. That decision would be based on Steve's new vision of what a change in suppliers will actually mean for Dumont. It could well be that this vision will support a price *increase,* not a discount. I have seen it happen many times.

Regardless, the "No" system guides Bill and protects him every step of the way, and it will do the same for you. In your personal and working life, you make all sorts of agreements every day. That is, you *negotiate.* These agreements—big and small—have as great an impact on your life as anything else. They drive your life, really. All of our lives. But how many of us approach these negotiations truly aware of what we're really doing? Very few. Often we get away with this easygoing or oblivious attitude, or so it seems. Sometimes we don't even know we are *in* a negotiation, let alone prepare for it—until it's too late. How many times have you experienced the panic that sets in after some rash decision or agreement you really didn't think about, or whose consequences you didn't realize? Show me the person who hasn't been blindsided when a negotiation has gone off the rails entirely. *What just happened! Now what should I do?*

Take my good friend Ralph, a developer who had invested his entire fortune in a project in California. In this region, conservation and protection of natural resources are very important to the community, and Ralph found himself up against a local council that he considered more than difficult; to him, they were impossible. As we enjoyed cocktails and the setting sun on my back deck, he unloaded on me with his woes dealing with what he perceived as a group of people driving him out of business.

"Ralph, what do they want?"

"To give me a hard time. To drive me out of the valley."

"No, seriously, what are they after?"

"Well, what do you mean, Jim?"

"This is a negotiation. What do they want from it? Something is driving them."

My friend mulled my question in silence and realized he had no idea what they wanted. As we sat on the deck he started making some wild guesses. I listened for a few minutes before I stopped him, stepped inside the house, and returned with a sheet of paper. On the spot, we started to build a plan. What was the long-term aim, the continuing task and responsibility of Ralph's development? What were the problems to be faced and overcome? What did the community hope to gain from this development? What did "their world" demand?

While Ralph knew what he wanted from the negotiation, that was about it. He had no idea what *they* wanted—the local council. He had no idea how to proceed when the situation got the least bit complicated. He had no thought process to guide his work—no solid plan to support and enhance his decisions. In fact, he had never even thought of negotiation as a series of decisions. Instead, he had been negotiating with his emotions—excitement, maybe some fear. He was burdened with unwarranted assumptions. His crystal ball was very cloudy, which is worse than no crystal ball at all. No wonder he got into trouble and hated to negotiate with that council.

Once Ralph discovered he could negotiate based on decisions and use "no" to his great advantage, he faced the council with greater skill and confidence. In the end, his real estate development was completed to the satisfaction of almost everyone. My purpose in this book is to provide you with the same new mindset that I provided for Ralph twenty years ago and still provide for my clients today. Negotiation is negotiation, whether it's

- handling a complex multimillion-dollar deal that could make or break a business

- submitting a career-building proposal to your boss
- gaining admission to the university of your choice
- settling a dispute with the pool contractor (or with the homeowner)
- getting your child to agree to go to bed
- getting that summer internship or landing that first job
- making progress during a dicey parent-teacher conference

Using my system, you can negotiate anything. No more hopes and prayers. No more fear and panic. You will know where you stand at all times and what to do next. No more guessing and unnecessary giving in. No wasted answers and offers, immediately regretted. You will understand any conflict or issue involving another human being as a negotiation you can reasonably control with planning and solid decision-making.

Chaos does *not* have to rule, in either your business or your everyday life. There is a much better way, and it's not rocket science. My "No" system is a set of clear principles and practices that you follow step by step by step. My system is for Mom, Dad, the kids, the entrepreneur, the professional corporate negotiator, the CEO, the teacher, the realtor, the banker, the politician, the carpenter, and the diplomat.

I want you to think about negotiation a little differently—a lot differently—and to see negotiation neither as a chore nor as a nightmare, but as a challenge you learn to enjoy. With "no," you have much control over the outcome. No more wondering, *What just happened! Now what should I do?* Those days are gone forever. You're safe now. Your back is covered.

◻   ◻   ◻

In order to understand the power of "no," you must first understand that "no" rejects the compromise- and assumption-driven reigning paradigm in negotiation today. If this makes you wince—after all, who doesn't want to "get to yes"—hang in for a few pages. The "No" system is not just contrarian. It creates an entirely new paradigm for negotiation—one that makes common sense, then intellectual sense, and finally practical sense in your life and work.

If you're a devotee of required compromise and endless assumptions, there are many businesspeople—I'm one of them—who have you for lunch every day. They have developed high-level strategies whose *only purpose* is to take advantage of your weak mindset of compromise and assumption. These tactics and strategies, I want you to know, accomplish their goal without too much trouble, grinding negotiators and their businesses into the dirt day in and day out. Think Steve and Dumont. My purpose with this book is to enable you to turn the tables on these folks. "No" will give you the upper hand over strategies like Steve's and all other negotiating strategies. Throughout these chapters I will include real-life stories of my clients achieving great success using my system. You'll see firsthand the powerful results produced by "no" every day.

For the fun of it, I sometimes introduce my system and the "no" principle with the story about the day I watched my granddaughter Lily negotiate with her mom over going to bed. I watched as three-year-old Lily said no to her mom five times and in the end got exactly what she wanted. Lily sure wasn't afraid to say no or hear no—she just kept negotiating. Persistence is important to the success of "no."

If you're a parent, you know that every child hears "no" as the *start* of the negotiation, not the *end* of it. As adults, however, we've been conditioned and trained to fear the word, so with audiences and clients I slowly and carefully go about proving that the practice of politely saying no, calmly hearing no, and just inviting no has a beneficial impact on any negotiation. In fact, the invitation for the other side to say no has an amazing power to bring down barriers and allow for solid beneficial communication. Giving someone permission to say no takes pressure off by lowering the intensity of emotions. Since the subject right now is children, let's say you're the parent walk-ing into a parent-teacher conference to discuss your child's lack of self-control and respect for authority. This could be a very tough meeting, with trouble possibly brewing. You've al-ready had a talk with Johnny and you have a plan to help solve this and get Johnny on the right track. You are here hoping to gain the teacher's help. This is a negotiation, plain and simple, and you should begin this exchange with a clear statement to the teacher that you have a plan and you want her to feel com-fortable rejecting your ideas. You want her to be comfortable in saying no. You would be well advised to say at the first oppor-tunity, "Mrs. Jones, I have noticed some restlessness in Johnny and I have a plan to solve this problem he is creating. I want you to feel comfortable rejecting the plan and feel free to give me your ideas. That said, my impression right now is that . . ."

This straightforward invitation for the teacher to say no al-lows him or her to feel comfortable and, if necessary, tell you what's really going on. And you must really mean this, because you probably don't know what's really going on at the school.

If you're the teacher, you might begin the conference by saying, "Mr. Smith, I don't know you well at all. I only know Johnny. He's a good boy, but I've been teaching twenty-three years, and his behavior at times does prompt some questions. May I ask them? Please, set me straight." This is a slightly more subtle invitation to "no"—and one the teacher should also mean. For both parent and teacher, the simple invited "no" is a liberation. Barriers come down immediately, making room for a concerted effort to solve the problem.

Back to business. Say your company is saddled with a terri-ble contract ginned up by a negotiator now long gone. You're losing money on every shipment under this deal. Something has to give. A plausible strategy is a phone call "right to the top" at the other company in which you say flat-out, "We did a terrible job negotiating with you. You probably knew that at the time. I didn't. Now I do. We can't continue this way; we're stuck. How can we fix this? When can you and I meet to discuss a solution?"

A lot of people would shy away from such a phone call, others will be flabbergasted at the very idea, but in fact it's the safest thing you can do. It's simply an honest statement of the situation. *No, we can't continue down the fatal path my former people put us on, but we can solve this problem. Let's talk.* And you know what? The other company will be happy to talk. Why? It's the most effective decision on their part if they want to keep your business.

I emphasize the power of "no" in order to emphasize that good negotiation is all about *making good decisions.* "No" gives you the new mindset with which to make good decisions in any negotiation whatsoever. With this principle opening the door, you are prepared to handle both the parent-teacher conference and the shipments that are losing money.

I want to be very clear: The "no" principle is *not* about intransigence. Just the opposite. It's about openness and honesty. The invitation to "no" tells everyone at the table that we're all adults here, so let's talk rationally. Let's slow things down. Let's take away the fear of failure. "No" allows everyone involved to put away the need to be right, to be the smartest, to be the strongest, or to be the toughest. It prevents you from making weak—and worse, bad—decisions because of your need to feel safe and secure and liked by the other side. "No" says to everyone at the table, *Let's bury any rush to judgment born of the getting-to-yes mentality. Relax,* "no" says, *I'm not trying to fleece you, and you're not about to fleece me.*

If you're having a hard time believing "no" really brings the barriers down and takes the air out of emotion, do me a favor. Try it. Mark your place right here and don't read another page until you get the opportunity, or can create the opportunity, to put "no" to a simple test—in the home, in the office, at school, at church, anywhere. Someone is going to ask you to do something or to come to an agreement on a topic or an issue or you can ask someone to do something or to agree with you. Just create a harmless little situation at the water cooler and say, "Gee, Jane, I can't do that, but tell me . . ." Or, "Now, Jane, if my suggestion doesn't work for you, please tell me no. You won't hurt my feelings. Really. I can handle it. Just tell me no."

You will *feel* the results instantly. Such a polite "no" does not offend people. On the contrary, it puts them at ease. It invites adult behavior (even from children). It opens the way for good decisions. After all my years coaching clients in every imaginable kind of negotiation, I can still be surprised by the almost magical power of "no." The word you have been trained to fear is, in fact, the word that will change your negotiating life forever.

"No" requires a solid, ironclad mission and purpose. It's a well-established idea in the business world, of course, but M&P (mission and purpose) in the "No" system takes on a contrarian meaning. It's not about you, but *them*—the other side.

The "No" system also makes you understand the dangers of neediness. Simply put, you do *not* need this deal, because neediness leads inexorably to unnecessary compromise. "No" will change you as a negotiator almost overnight—and for the better—and so will the idea of building vision in the other party ("How much risk of failure can Dumont absorb with a new, unproven widget, Steve?"), the instructions about creating agendas that really work, and the lessons on how to ask good questions and how to listen to the answers.

Which sounds better to you, good decisions or rampaging emotions? Confidence or neediness? Good questions or unwarranted assumptions and expectations? Concentrating on actions you can control or chasing results you cannot control?

Getting what you want is as easy as saying no.

❐   ❐   ❐

Long before I became a professional negotiation coach I was a pilot, first military, then commercial. That's where I learned the importance of using systems to manage and perform complex activities. Without systems, you can't fly a plane safely, that's for sure. If you've ever peered into the cockpit as you file through the door of a commercial jet—and who hasn't?—you've probably observed the pilots working through their mandatory checklists printed on heavy plastic cards. This is how they monitor and enforce the system. (If you ever crawl into a private plane and the pilot does *not* go through a checklist before starting the engine, you might consider deplaning on the spot. Seriously. "Feet first" beats the alternative every time.)

Not long ago, a lawyer in Cleveland, a self-styled student of negotiation, read my first book, *Start with No,* and sent it to his daughter, a student at Notre Dame. She liked it so much she enrolled in one of my training programs, during which one of our coaches worked with her in academics and coached her on her negotiation to get one of the prized internships in the White House. A key component of the preparation was the checklist for the all-important interview in Washington. On the big day, she flew in, sat down, used her checklist, and got the job practically on the spot. I wasn't surprised. Her story and thousands like it are the reason I still use checklists in negotiations just as diligently as I did as a pilot.

Negotiation is a complex beast. There's a lot going on. Checklists keep it all under control. They give us such a tremendous advantage, such ease of mind. I will use them throughout this book, and I will teach you how to use them in your negotiations. In the last chapter I introduce the "short form" of the Checklist and Log that my clients use to manage their negotiations all over the world.

Another feature running throughout the book will be tips for "test driving" the most straightforward principles and activities. I've already invited you to find a simple water-cooler situation with which to try out "no." That was a test drive. There will be quite a few others—quick, simple ways to try things out in fairly risk-free situations. I have no fear of losing you in a negotiation wreck. You might dent a fender, I guess, but you'll also learn that "no" works, that certain specific kinds of questions work, and that a specific kind of agenda works.

In the end, I will not only change the way you perhaps think now about negotiating—out with "yes," in with "no"—but I will give you the know-how, the how-to, and the actual tools with which to make it all happen. For any student, businessperson, or professional, for parents, children, homeowners, landlords, tenants, employees, employers, debtors, creditors, buyers, sellers—for anyone negotiating anything—*this system works.*

1

Stop the Roller Coaster, I Want to Get Off

Controlling the Commotion of Emotion

Before you make a decision, your emotions rage all over the place. Then when you make a decision, you set about rationalizing it. When you watch yourself and other people carefully, you can actually see the transition from one emotional state to the next—from the emotional state to the decision state. Every day, every hour, even every minute, under some circumstances, you flip back and forth, back and forth. *I want to change my career. I just do, even though I'm doing well right here. My dad says I shouldn't. I know I probably shouldn't. But I want to.* We've all had such experiences. *I want to buy this car. I know I shouldn't. Yeah, I will.* Back and forth, on issues big and small. Sometimes this dynamic is plain for all to see. Sometimes it's almost all underground. Regardless, it is always there.

Successful negotiation of any sort requires that you understand this fact and use it. As I have already emphasized in the introduction, your overriding task as a negotiator—in the office or in the home, with your family, or anywhere at all—is to replace compromise- and fear-based negotiating with decision-based negotiating. You must learn to progress from raw, unexamined emotions, which never produce good agreements, to the careful decisions that eventually do. Most negotiators remain mired in their own emotions. Nor do they ever get past the emotions that are bogging the other side down. You must see the emotions on *both* sides for what they are and work with them, not against them. When you do, you're way ahead of the game and way ahead of 99 percent of your fellow men and women. But it's hard not to get trapped in the emotional realm, especially because of one particular emotion that dominates all others in negotiations: *neediness*.

EXHIBIT NO. 1: NEEDINESS

Why are the eyes of so many beasts like the big cats, grizzly bears, polar bears, and wolverines set in the front of the head, facing forward? Because these animals are *predators* always looking ahead for prey. They have no need to look back or even much to the side. They have their eyes on the prize, because this is how they make their living. Now, why are our own eyes also set in the front of the head, facing forward? Because we are predators as well. Watching children in a playground is delightful, but it is also cautionary, as every parent knows, because along with the friendships and the kindnesses we also see some king-of-the-hill, one-upmanship, bullying instincts emerge at an early age. For many, these instincts last a lifetime, as anyone who has spent much time in a nursing home knows. They accompany some of us right to the grave. (You've probably seen the ad on TV with the two sets of grandparents sending pictures of their grandchildren back and forth, trying to one-up each other. The scene is played for laughs, but it also says a lot about human nature.)

Our "one-upping," predatory nature is a harsh truth and not always a welcome one. But it is a vitally necessary point for you to understand. Like it or not, we are predators by nature, and the first instinct of predators is to take advantage of the fear-racked, the distressed, the vulnerable—in one word, the needy. We humans, at least, are also capable of wonderful altruism, but we don't see much altruism in the world of business and negotiation, despite all the sweet talk of cagey practitioners.

In a negotiation, you may be dealing with some serious predators who are looking for the slightest sign of distress and neediness. "Dog-eat-dog" may not do justice to the aggression you will encounter, and good negotiators pounce on the slightest appearance of weakness. Every time you leave a long-winded message on an answering machine providing all kinds of information, you put yourself at a disadvantage. How? You're too anxious and therefore seem needy. Each time you answer a question with much more information than is really called for, you are showing neediness and putting yourself at risk. Every time you set a price and then lower it, you are showing need and putting yourself in a weaker position. By cutting your price without being asked to and then explaining why you felt it important to cut the price, you are showing neediness and reinforcing a bad habit.

Many business negotiators are expert in *creating* neediness by feeding the hopes and expectations of the other side. They paint rosy, exaggerated scenarios for year-making commissions and career-making deals—all for the purpose of building neediness on the part of the other side for this bonanza. Then, when the neediness is well established, they lower the boom with changes, exceptions, and a host of other demands. And why not? They have the upper hand.

These are not profound observations about neediness. They are common sense, when you stop to think about them. The problem is that all too often we do not stop to think about neediness. Many trained negotiators schooled at our finest institutions have never heard a discussion of the subject, let alone considered how to deal with neediness. I know this because I've lectured at these institutions. The students understand what I'm talking about immediately—who wouldn't?—but they have no sense of how neediness plays out over the course of a negotiation. Certainly most people don't watch out for neediness during the negotiations encountered in their daily lives. But you must. When you slip and allow yourself to appear needy you are in danger and your negotiation is in big trouble.

YOU DO *NOT* NEED THIS DEAL

Today, in our wealthy society, most of us have no good reason to *need* much of anything, but somehow we fool ourselves and program our minds and make statements like "I *need* this leather jacket." Or "I *need* this Maserati." Or "I *need* to make this call." Or "I *need* to talk to you." Or "I *need* this opportunity." Or "I *need* this deal." Or "I *need* to see her." We use the word "need" much too casually.

You're negotiating for a new home? You love this one house so much you *need* it? It's perfect — perfect neighborhood, school district, size, color, fixtures, garage, game room, everything? You have to have it? You've decided for sure? In the first place, do you really need it? It's not your family or your career. It is, bottom line, a shelter with four walls (probably more) and a roof. There are others. In the second place, who says the seller is not the one with some real neediness to make this deal? Control your own neediness. If, after all the looking at houses, you decide to pay a $100,000 premium, at least you've clearly understood what you're doing, *and why.* (Clearly, auctions are expressly designed to build and manipulate dueling buyers' respective neediness. Beware.)

You do truly need the basics of physical survival — air, water, food, clothing, and shelter — and everyone reading this book already has these. You also need the basics of intellectual and emotional well-being for a well-lived life of love, family, friendship, satisfying work, hobbies, and faith — each reader has his or her own list here. But it's a *short* list, and it does not —

or should not—include the $500 jacket or the $100,000 car, because there are other jackets and other cars. Nor should the list include this particular job, deal, or agreement, because there are other jobs, deals, and agreements.

You do *not* need this agreement. Nevertheless, neediness is everywhere. Sometimes it is blatant and easy to spot, but just as often it is subtle and insidious.

Test Drive Take ten minutes at the end of the day and assess your actions and your conversations, looking for signs of neediness. No one knows better than you when it's sneaking into the picture. Honest appraisal will uncover it. Did you talk too much or too fast in a conversation, negotiation, or interview, maybe to make just the right impression? Jot this neediness down.

- Did you leave long-winded messages? Jot it down.
- Did you make the direct statement "I need this or that"? Jot it down.
- Did you get excited and start looking ahead at the thought of some success, great or small? Jot it down.
- When you're finished making your list, think carefully about the *real* motivation behind each item—not the apparent motivation or the rationalized motivation, but the *real* one. See if you can identify the neediness.

The list of our needs is endless. Our passion for the perfect house? It includes just a wee bit of neediness to demonstrate to the world our financial success, doesn't it? The dueling grandparents sending pictures of the grandkids in the TV ad? There's some neediness in that scenario, too: the neediness to be seen as winning grandparents with successful children who are in turn rearing these incredible grandchildren.

This is the way we are—and in our everyday lives, so what?

But in negotiation it's a different story. In negotiation, neediness is a killer. People who understand this—who see the big ways and little ways people express neediness—use this understanding to great advantage.

Te s t   D r i v e   After you have identified your own signs of neediness on a given day, look around your world and find the signs in others: the people who talked too much in an effort to please you, who needed to be right all the time, who needed to win at all costs, who needed to be the center of attention. If you look, you'll find the neediness.

It is very easy to slip into such a state of neediness, often without even being aware of it. Think about something as simple as a greeting.

> *Hi, I'm Betty Jones.*
> *Hello, Ms. Jones.*

Such subtle subservience could put you at an immediate disadvantage in an important negotiation. Such a response concedes that Ms. Jones is top gun in this room, and she will know it. You could be ripe for the picking. So call her Betty instead.

Consider this appeal for an appointment:

> *Ms. Smith, this is Bob Harris. I'm with First*
> *Advantage Venture Fund, and I want to see if I*
> *could get ten minutes on your calendar so I can*
> *show you how we can work with you in the future.*

Remember, start-up companies aren't the only parties who can be needy. Some start-ups are well funded and choosy regarding any venture capitalist they may bring in. Investors can also get into the needy mode, just as Bob Harris did while more or less *begging* for this appointment. It leaves a poor first impression. Bob should have said, "Hi, Jill, my name is Bob Harris.

I'm not quite sure that we as a venture fund fit where you're going. I just don't know. What I'd like to do is meet with you so we can see where you're going and you can look at where we're going at First Advantage and see if there might be a fit. When's the best time on your calendar?"

No neediness in this approach. Just a calm proposal accompanied by a quiet invitation for Jill to say "no thanks" if she happens to have all the capital she requires.

Or say you're "negotiating" for your first job. This is a big deal. (I know. My daughter Kristi is embarking on her first job search as I write this paragraph. I remember the equivalent moments in the lives of the other kids. I remember it in my own life. It's a big deal, and it is a *negotiation*.) You have college loans on which the first payment is due in six months. You want to prove your worthiness to your parents and your family—and yourself. And this job you're interviewing for is the perfect job in the perfect part of the country. You're losing sleep over this amazing opportunity. You are overwhelmed with enthusiasm. You are eager and accept the very first appointment time. You spend hours preparing statements about how valuable you would be to this organization. In the interview itself, you sit forward in your chair, talk a little fast, start answering before the interviewers can even finish the questions.

Tell me Harold, in school did you—?

Oh, I loved school, I really enjoyed accounting and finance, I found I was really good in those areas and I really enjoyed my professors.

Tell me something about—

I just love your company and the work that you do, I really think I am a perfect fit. I grew up just down the street and I know a lot about your company and its customers. I have watched all the changes and it is just amazing how far it has come.

What is your—?

I am very strong in people skills and am a very talented listener who can focus on the issues at hand.

How many—?

I have completed almost thirty percent of the work toward my MBA and I plan to finish part-time while working for you.

What's going on here? Harold's neediness to land this job is killing his thought process and ruining his chances. He's not thinking about the challenges facing the company—he's not even thinking about why the company decided to interview him. He's practically screaming "neediness," and the interviewer will not be impressed. Think about it. Imagine that you have invited this young man or woman to discuss working for you and all he or she talks about is how good he or she is, what his or her plans are, and what he or she sees as his or her greatest strength. How in the world do you hire someone like that? If you're like me, you're much more likely to consider someone who wants to know about your company and the opportunity you offer. You want someone who's calm, cool, and collected. You might not have put the issue in these terms before now, but you want someone who's not *so darned needy*.

The next time you watch one of the predator-prey nature shows on public television or one of the wildlife channels, watch the chase scenes carefully. There are always one or two in which the lion or the cheetah is not successful, and each time the scenario is the same: The predator gets closer to the antelope . . . closer . . . closer, then slips back slightly—and *immediately* gives up. On the spot. When the distance to the prey begins to widen, the hunter quits. She will never waste energy on what's shaping up as a losing cause. She saunters off, because it doesn't matter. There are other wildebeest, other gazelles. Likewise, the trained negotiator has no needs, because it just doesn't matter. In this economy, there are other deals.

There are other jobs for our first-time job searcher. Be ready to turn the page on this job, this deal. Let it go. Being overanxious and needy is not going to get it for you anyway.

Perhaps the negotiation in which the neediness dynamic is most powerful and dangerous is the retail sales negotiation, in which the golden rule of business is the implicit understanding of both sides that "the one with the gold rules." The buyer has the gold, and his or her self-image is enhanced by buying and consuming as much as he or she can. In the West we see ourselves as buyers, don't we? We proudly buy and consume as much as we can. The salesperson, on the other hand, is definitely the dependent party in the negotiation. Historically, the salesperson has a problem with his or her self-image. The very term "sales" is being replaced in many fields by "business development," because the image of the "salesperson" is that of the huckster on the street, almost. Moreover, the salesperson must be prepared to give, to compromise, to please, while the buyer takes everything he or she can get. After all, the buyer can go elsewhere, in most cases, but the poor seller *needs* this deal.

I first experienced the advantage of the buyer while working as a kid at the Stanley's family-owned fruit and vegetable stand in Washington, Pennsylvania. I was a strong kid and helped out wherever possible, unloading the truck coming in from the market, filling pecks of potatoes by hand, stacking pop bottles, filling egg cartons. One day the owner, Wade Stanley (who we all called Mr. Wade), honored me by asking me to travel with him to purchase the wholesale produce for the fruit stand for the week. As we were driving to Pittsburgh on Rt. 19 (just after midnight), he laid out our plan. I was to be the "taster," and my job was to frown and shake my head regardless how good the fruit tasted. Mr. Wade stressed how important it was for me to show no interest in anything until the purchase was made—and not even then, preferably. No rushing to judgment by exclaiming how great this apple was; no rushing to close the deal, because nothing was more likely to blow our chance of getting the lowest price in these negotiations. Mr. Wade understood this. I didn't—not really, but I didn't have to. All I had to do was eat and frown.

And so I did, as we walked from stand to stand. I must have tasted a dozen different fruits, and each time, I frowned and shook my head no. Before I knew it, dawn was breaking and Mr. Wade was in high gear. A couple of times he started walking away from sellers until he finally had the prices he wanted. After we had our produce and were driving back to Washington, Mr. Wade explained his negotiating strategy, and pretty much in the same terms I now use—terms of neediness. My frowning as I tasted and his willingness to walk away were all for the purpose of building the sellers' neediness. The longer the process took, the more likely the sellers would start feeling neediness and would complete this negotiation on terms favorable to us, the buyers.

The rule could not be simpler: If there is any need in this negotiation, it has to be theirs, not yours.

Perhaps you saw the movie (or the David Mamet play) *Glengarry Glen Ross*. Dapper, calm, and totally under control, Alec Baldwin (in the movie) manages a team of salesmen by demanding that they always drive hard to close the deal for land at two new developments, Glengarry and Glen Ross. Alec is cool and confident and makes sure his salespeople see his Rolex and other accoutrements of success. If they can close, they, too, can have all this. No neediness from Alec Baldwin, the boss, but he builds his team's neediness without mercy. They began to sweat, literally, out of neediness for deals and success. Jack Lemmon's character can't handle it; he's a basket case. This is a strong story, but it has one gaping hole in the plot. All of this neediness Baldwin is building in his sales force will *not* yield more sales for his people.

Go get 'em, gang! Make something happen! Go for the jugular! Close, close, close! Many unfortunate salespeople have been exhorted with such drivel for their entire careers. It's painful to see, because such urgent "closing" betrays neediness. In fact, the "close, close, close" mentality is probably the best illustration I can offer of the dangers of neediness. When someone has tried to seal an agreement with you too quickly—and someone has, in one context or another, unless you're still a babe in arms—you instinctively reacted in the negative, didn't you? Nothing, but nothing, will blow a negotiation faster than such a rush to judgment, because the recipient of that rush—the buyer, the customer—immediately has a vision of neediness on the other side, which is unsettling by itself and also serves as a warning to look closer at this deal. This is why there is no way Alec Baldwin's sales force can thrive when their neediness for the sale is so flagrant it probably smells (literally, from the sweat).

I therefore have a different rule: No closing.

WATCH YOUR LANGUAGE

Talking is often an overt showing of need. Therefore this rule:

No talking.

I exaggerate, of course, in order to make the point that talking and neediness often go hand in hand. Many people have an apparently insatiable desire to make sure their voice is heard. After all, you're bright and it's human nature to want people to know that you are. That is, you need to feel important. *Okay,* think some of the shrewder people you deal with: *We'll be happy to let you feel important as we skin you alive.*

Thomas Edison, one of the greatest inventors of all time, was also a master negotiator, with the help of the Colonel, a business associate. There was once a meeting set up by the Colonel in his office. Three people were present: the Colonel, Edison the genius, and a banker whom the Colonel thought might want to buy Edison's latest amazing invention, the ticker-tape machine that would provide Wall Street with quotes directly from the floor of the New York Stock Exchange. Thomas

Edison's presentation could not have been simpler: He set up
the machine and turned it on. Then he stepped away and let it
run. The banker was left on his own to read the tape, and of
course he understood the value of this contrivance instantly.
The Colonel asked the man what he thought. "It is a decent development," the banker replied. "I'll give you $5,000 for it."

Now, Edison had already decided that he would let his machine do the talking in this negotiation. A valid and very wor-
thy goal. Hearing the offer, he just tightened his mouth in a
negative way but said nothing. "All right," said the investor,
"$10,000." Edison declined to comment. So did the Colonel.
With the silence filling the room, the investor said, "Okay,
$25,000!" This time Edison reacted with bewilderment but
said not a word. The investor declared that Edison was trying
to fleece him. He would pay $100,000 and not one penny
more. Edison looked at the Colonel, who nodded in affirma-
tion, and Edison accepted with a frown. The banker laughed
and said in celebration, "Edison, I would have paid $150,000!"
Edison smiled and replied, "I would have taken $10,000!"

I love this story! It could be used to illustrate practically
every single principle in my system, as I'll point out in the
pages that follow. As proof positive of the power of keeping
our mouths shut, it's in a class of its own. Compulsive talking is
a common issue that hard-driving types have to watch out for
at all times. They need to know it all, or, short of that (probably), they need to be seen to know it all. The adrenaline kicks
in, the neediness becomes a biochemical fact, then the neediness becomes a biochemical addiction. It's true.

Again: Control your own neediness
while you look for and build theirs.

Edison sat quietly, controlling his talking and his neediness,
allowing the banker's neediness to mount higher and higher
and higher. Alec Baldwin's sales force in *Glengarry Glen Ross*
would have had a great deal more success had they controlled

their own neediness and their endless chatter while building the neediness of the potential buyers by calmly and politely allowing the beauties of their developments to speak volumes. But then this wouldn't have been much of a story, would it?

How many people do you know who won't let you get a word in edgewise? By being overbearing, these people are actually betraying neediness. Needy outgoing messages on answering machines abound these days. Instead of the normal "Hi, this is . . . Please leave your message at the beep," these folks greet callers with a detailed message regarding their busy schedules for the hour, the day, and the week. And we can imagine what kind of messages they leave on other people's answering machines: long ones. Do you see what's going on here? These folks need to make sure we understand how busy they are, how competent they are, and how lucky we will be if they can spare us the time of day. But it's all counterproductive.

One of the most effective life insurance salesmen I ever met was a man in a wheelchair who could not speak. He used a marker and a board to communicate, patiently writing out his questions. I would not wish this man's disability on anyone, but his only means of asking questions was a terrific advantage in his profession, as he was the first to acknowledge, because it's hard to be needy while sitting in a wheelchair calmly writing out questions by hand. (His most effective question, by the way, was, "If we lose you, where will your family live?")

Test Drive Sit down at a meeting with the following note placed inconspicuously in front of you: "No talking. Listen." Now simply *talk less* than you normally would. Instead, listen more and listen better. Focus intently on what you're hearing. If you struggle—and you may, because listening is a lot harder than most people imagine—take notes. You'll be pleasantly surprised with the results. There's no downside. Then do this again and again and again and again—listen, listen, listen to what people are telling you. Then let it become a habit.

Now think for a moment about "cold calls" and "warm calls," because they're the ultimate lesson on this subject. Just thinking about cold calls gives the average businessperson chills. It's tough, no doubt about it, and a lot of fine people just won't do it. Cold-calling is the worst way to do business. We all know that. But I say it's also the most important way to be able to do business. Why? In the very worst business environment, if you can successfully cold-call, you can always get a job. More important, however—more basic—is that cold-calling is a great training ground for negotiation, period, and it can be surprisingly effective *because your neediness is under control.* You have no great expectations, that's for sure, and your discipline is keen.

You should start off by saying something like "Well, Mary, I have no idea whether what we do has any relevance for you and your business. I just don't know; maybe it doesn't. If not, just tell me and I'll be on my way, but if whoever handles your market research . . ."

And off you go—or not. You have given Mary permission to say no. Your neediness is under control. Really, a cold call is just another negotiation—no more and no less—and by the end of this book you'll understand how to handle one according to the same rules and habits with which you would handle any other negotiation.

Now consider the warm call.

Hey, Tom, this is Bill. Man, do I have a hot one. I told them all about you. They're on the tee. They're ready. All you gotta do is call and collect. You owe me one, buddy.

Oh, yeah? Hearing this, Tom's blood is probably racing, but if he's not careful he might be better off with a cold call than with a referral like this one. If he's not careful, he'll lose discipline, start thinking about the payday, get excited, become needy. He'll start this warm call by blurting, "Hey, Dominic, Bill told me to give you a call. You're in the market for a new car. I have just the one for you." Before Tom can go any further, what is Dominic thinking? "Boy, that Bill has a big mouth. Now I have to deal with this yahoo friend of his. Last time I'll ever tell Bill I'm looking for anything." Into the phone he says, "What did you say your name was? Tom? Well, Tom, our mutual friend Bill has misled you, but thanks for the call."

In just this way has the earnest Tom snatched defeat from the jaws of victory. He should have said to Dominic, "Hello. My name is Tom and I am not sure that what I am doing fits. If it doesn't, please just let me know and I'll get off the phone. Is that fair? Dominic, I am in the auto industry and I have an auto that if you have any interest in may be a perfect fit for you."

Do yourself a favor: Treat every warm call as though it's the most frigid one you ever made. Don't show neediness. Don't feel neediness. Stick to your system. When you feel emotions starting to run hot and heavy in a negotiation—maybe a warm call, maybe not—slow down. The high-pitched voice is a sure sign of need. The rushed delivery is another sure sign. While needy negotiators raise their voices, negotiators under control lower their voices. So lower your voice in times of inner turmoil. Take it easy. You do not need this deal.

DON'T WORRY ABOUT REJECTION

Many people live in fear of rejection, and what is this fear, bottom line? It's the need to be liked. If you don't need to be liked, you have no fear of rejection. If you have no fear of rejection, you can say no when it's called for. When you negotiate, it is imperative to understand just what rejection is and who can reject you—and who cannot.

The people on the other side of the table
cannot **reject you.**

Why not? Because you don't need anything from them. Nothing. So how can they reject you? It's impossible. The parent can reject the child, because the child certainly needs the parent. The spouse can reject the spouse. The teacher can even reject the student in the early grades, when the boy or girl truly does need this teacher. But can the adults on the other side of the table in a negotiation really reject you? No, they don't have any such power. Never allow them to believe that they do.

You must understand that you cannot go out into the world spending emotional energy in the effort to be liked, to be smart, or to be important. This is all just wasteful and dangerous neediness, often enough because of a fear of being rejected. You want to be recognized as being effective and businesslike— that's all. You want to spend your energy on the task of business. You have no need for the rest of it. But how often I have seen negotiators fall into this particular neediness trap!

In labor-management disputes, it happens all the time. In fact, a common tactic of management is to find employees who want a boost to the ego and can be made to feel critically important to a successful conclusion. These employees are just itching for the chance to say (or imply) to their fellow union members, "If it wasn't for me this contract would not have happened. I saved this contract and this union." Because what matters to them is their importance in the negotiation—their *need* for this feeling—such employees are easy pickings for management and can be manipulated until they are double agents, often acting as messengers for management. Say the union members are balking over a proposed pay cut. They don't believe it's truly necessary or that management will hang tough on the issue. Management uses a delegate who needs to be important and plants a false message, which the delegate then takes back to his or her members: "Our committee is getting us killed. I've got buddies in management. What they're telling me is that they might shut this plant down if we keep on like this." I've seen how this can happen.

The time was in the 1970s, when a very famous airline with a billion dollars in the bank was set to expand its routes around the world. To accomplish this goal, it could either build from within, buying airplanes and hiring employees as needed at a controlled pace, or it could buy an almost bankrupt existing airline and its few airplanes and many employees, hundreds of whom had been laid off for years. To my mind, quite clearly, growing from within would produce great commercial success for the company while also producing job growth, pay increases, healthy careers, and security for the employees and their families. The second choice—acquiring the troubled second airline—was the road to ruin, including career stagnation at best, layoffs quite probably. Within the employee base were senior employees who, like the very top management, would be unaffected by either choice. They would get theirs, regardless, and it was within this group that management nurtured the need to feel important. Then management used these needy employees to convince the rank and file to believe that the long-term positive good of the company required *not* controlled growth but the roll of the loaded dice and the acquisition of the second airline.

Management played its hand perfectly. The unwitting senior employees played a major role in convincing the junior employees that this acquisition was the best way forward. The rest is history. I cannot name the companies involved, but I'm sure some readers will know who they are. In short order, hundreds of the younger employees of the successful airline were laid off. Those who did keep their jobs lost ground. Eight years after the acquisition, the merged airline declared bankruptcy and was sold for pennies on the dollar. And it had been inevitable from the beginning.

This is an issue I feel strongly about, as I suppose is clear. I can't begin to count the times I've seen negotiating team members undermine their own team in a host of ways, almost always because of neediness. They leak valuable information; they break their team's discipline by discussing important points of interest that all had agreed not to discuss; and they urge unnecessary financial terms and compromises—all because clever negotiators on the other side of the table manipulate their need to be smart, to be liked, and to be important.

Take Bob, the CEO of his company, who had a driving desire to also become chairman of the board. As CEO Bob had done a great job of bringing new products to market and placing those products into the very largest end users in the industry. He had worked hard to help each board member see the value of his becoming chairman. The deal he struck with his board was that if he could bring the largest potential client in the industry into line as a paying customer, he would be moved into the chairman's seat when the current chairman retired in eight months. To open the negotiations with this giant client, Bob insisted that a deal must be one they couldn't refuse. So his opening offer to this giant included almost $10 million in free spare parts and service, which was something he had never even thought of doing before. The deal did go through. But anyway you cut it, Bob's need for a deal to use as a stepping stone to the chairmanship made him agree to a totally unnecessary and unasked-for compromise. The eventual deal camouflaged that compromise, but that's what it was.

I have even seen a company lose a deal because its neediness had led it to compromise *in every way imaginable:* four times on terms, three times on price, and I didn't know how many times on how many other issues before I came into the picture as their coach. To help them out of the hole they were in and to get back to profitability, I recommended they break off negotiations, regroup, and come back at full price. The quality of their product justified it. Full price was a fair price. I recommended they admit that with the terms and pricing as they were—discounted to the max—the company might not even be able to deliver. Top management did not agree with me. One executive explained that this was, at worst, a break-even deal, and any change from the current track of "being a good partner" would damage the "relationship" with the other company. They would lose all credibility as a viable supplier.

Okay, I said, if you don't want to work toward a profitable outcome, what's the plan? The plan was simple: Secure the relationship at any cost. At the end of the day (a long day; many months), my clients stayed their course. Then they got the shock of their lives: The beneficiary of all this need-induced negotiation *walked away* from this steal of a deal. In the post-mortem, they candidly explained that they sensed something was wrong. There was no push back. Whatever they asked for they got. *Why did they give in so easily on price and everything else?* (Something must be wrong, they correctly believed.) *What don't we know? What are they hiding? They have a great product, but can they be trusted to deliver on time? If they're selling their product at cost, barely, will they have the resources to build a next-generation product to take us into the future?*

And those inquiring executives were right. The always capitulating company would never have been able to make good on the commitments negotiated in that deal. The negotiators had been ridiculously, unnecessarily needy. And it happens all the time, with negotiations large and small.

WANTING IS FINE

As a negotiator aspiring to excellence, you must, at all costs, avoid showing need. In order to avoid showing need, you must never *feel* it. I cannot say this enough:

You do *not* need this deal.

Now, what happens if we simply substitute the word and the emotion "want" for "need"? The dynamics change, don't they? What picture comes to mind when you read the words "I want"? I see a yacht, specifically a 67-foot Viking convertible with a 3,000-mile range and three staterooms. What is your picture? As good negotiators, the word "want" means something we will work for, strive for, and plan for, but it is never confused with "need." Sure I *want* this Viking yacht that can take my family to Europe, but I hardly *need* it. Sure I want this global alliance with Humongous, Inc., but I don't need it. I want the house, but I don't need it. It will be their loss, not mine, if any of these deals falls through. Either way, I'll sleep tonight and I'll eat tomorrow.

You only *want* this deal.

"Need" is death; "want" is life. Believe me, this different attitude will make all the difference in your negotiating life. It will be instantly perceived and sensed by the folks on the other side of the table. Confidence and trust go up across the board. Control and discipline go up for you.

HOWEVER . . .

Sometimes, however, the need is real. Usually it is exaggerated, but not always. A classic example from history is the story of the Pilgrims at Plymouth Rock and that first winter. They needed help to survive, they knew it, and they were prepared to negotiate to gain that help. And they did negotiate with the Native Americans for help in clearing the land, preparing the ground, and planting maize. Then came the first Thanksgiving.

Sometimes the Pilgrims *were* needy, plain and simple. Sometimes they really were desperate for shelter, food, and supplies. Likewise, when the neediness is real for you, accept the fact and deal with it then and there in any negotiation. Quite often, the best strategy may be to reveal this neediness to the other party. That's right. Put it on an agenda to be discussed. (You will see how these agendas work in a later chapter.)

You've been looking for a job for six months and here, at long last, is a pretty good possibility? Unless you're super-human, you're going to have some neediness. You must acknowledge this to yourself and incorporate it into your strategy for the salary negotiation. You might even end up saying to the potential employer, "I like this company, and I'm great for the job. We're perfect for each other. But I have a problem. I *need* this job. I'm not going to kid you. And this is tough for me, because the salary you're offering is a bit low for the industry, and it's just not enough for my family, either. I'm in a bind."

On the other side of the desk, the prospective employer's first instinct may be to bury you: *Take this salary or shove off.* But by exposing your own neediness so frankly, you have presented a problem that could be mutually solved in the negotiation. By acknowledging your neediness you give yourself an opportunity to get your prospective employer to see your value and to pay for it. (You "build vision," a topic to be discussed.)

What does the employer require for this position? How important is it? What will your excellent performance bring to the organization? By identifying your salary problem but immediately moving into the employer's world to get him or her to see your value, you may be able to solve your problem. Or maybe not. The salary offer may not budge. If it doesn't, you have a difficult decision to make. In any event, there was no downside in stating the problem, and a very possible upside.

Say you're the pool contractor who really does need the second check from the homeowner. Your best suppliers are making nasty threats. Lose their goodwill and their willingness to do business with you, and you lose a lot. If you're convinced the homeowner does have the money and is happy with your work but simply does not want to pay right now, for whatever perverse reason, you may well have to lay your need on the table. *Sam, I can handle my employees right now, but my suppliers are another story. They want their money. I need to pay them—and I can't do that until you pay me. Those are large bills, as you know. How can I help you see the importance of my paying my suppliers? What happens to your pool and its finish date without suppliers?*

Those two simple questions are a start. I'll return to this saga later.

FEELING OKAY—AND UN-OKAY

Abraham Lincoln was a tall, lanky, homely man, with a nose too large and a neck too thin. As history tells it, he grew his beard at the recommendation of a young girl who believed it would make him more distinguished-looking. She was right. The beard helped, but he was still an odd sight. He always looked tired (and during the war he was—totally exhausted; he often spent hours visiting military hospitals in both the North and the South, giving comfort to the wounded). This was the president whom men and women, from both the Union and the Confederacy, called Abe, Father Abraham, Honest Abe, or Uncle Abe.

Now from the sublime to the ridiculous, but bear with me for a paragraph. In the end, my point will be crucial for a negotiator. Remember the old TV series *Columbo*? Or perhaps you occasionally watch the reruns in syndication. As a homicide detective in L.A., Columbo wears the raggedy trench coat, drives the beat-up Peugeot, tells witnesses heartwarming stories about his wife and his dog (a sad-looking basset hound, I believe, but definitely not a silky-sleek golden retriever), and has the habit of forgetting to ask a key question in every interview and interrogation. He has to ring the doorbell again, apologize, and ask that final question. He always presents himself as a little less competent than whomever he is interviewing and a little less than perfect—or, usually, a lot less than perfect. He could get his witnesses and even suspects to talk to him because he made *them* feel superior and therefore comfortable. And it was all an act on his part.

Likewise, Lincoln's inelegant appearance was no accident.

He understood in his bones that in order to lead the people he had to be trusted by the people. And he was. His office at the White House was always open. He took in all visitors, rich and poor, and treated them the same. His grasp of the English language was incomparable, but he never came across as speaking *down* to anyone. He spoke to *and believed* that everyone was a person with value, in essence. In today's loaded term, Lincoln belonged to no "elite." Also in today's lingo (made famous by the book *I'm Okay, You're Okay*), both he and Columbo seduced other people into feeling "okay." How did they do this? In each case, by using their own physical appearance and demeanor to be seen as *not-okay*. I truly believe Abraham Lincoln saved the Union because of this very human trait. Without it, the people and the soldiers would never have followed him through those agonizing years of war.

To be okay is to feel comfortable and therefore safe. That's the simplest way to define the word as it's used in pop psychology. From the moment of birth, all of us, as members of the human race, struggle to feel comfortable and safe. As a baby and a toddler, you demand—you need—the unconditional love of your parents that is the only source of your comfort and safety. As a young child, your demands in this regard increase. You want to be recognized. You want to be heard. You want to be liked. You want to be right. Or should I say you *need* all this? I'm afraid so. And this *need* to feel okay follows us right through adolescence (and how!) and right into adulthood, as we struggle for recognition, confirmation, achievement, success, and victory.

When called upon to appear in public or before your peers, are you looking forward to revealing your weaknesses? No, never. You need to put your strengths and assets on display. Maybe your strength is your knowledge, or physical beauty, or charming personality. Maybe you are cunning and fearless or quick of wit. Whatever your strength, that is what you instinctively build on. That is what you show the world. That is what you need to show the world.

Likewise, you compare yourself with others in order to see how you stack up. Are you a little ahead or a little behind? When you are with people you think you are ahead of, or at least equal to, you feel comfortable. Conversation comes easily and questions seem to have no risk. You feel okay. But in the presence of people to whom you feel inferior, whether culturally, socially, or intellectually, you feel not quite okay and can become defensive, aggressive, resentful, or a lot of other emotions. When someone looks perfect while you need a haircut, how do you feel? Exactly: a little uneasy, a little not-okay. Conversation may be difficult, questions seem full of risk, and you fear you will look silly or even stupid.

Turning the situation around, have you noticed how we humans tend to feel okay when we see someone who's *not*-okay? You feel okay when you see someone who doesn't quite measure up in some way. Soap opera fans watch the shows because the lives of those fictional characters are even more messed up than the viewers' own lives! You revel in the trials and tribulations of the rich and famous because now the tables are turned: a lot of good their fame and fortune has brought them! Suddenly you're more okay than the movie star forced to check into the $2,000-a-day rehab center, more okay than the movie star booked on shoplifting charges, more okay than the brilliant megastar who makes a fool of himself by being drunk and getting arrested. This is not your most attractive feature, perhaps, but there it is. Long ago the Germans gave it the name *schadenfreude*.

As with my observations about neediness, these about okayness are not revolutionary. I don't think anyone would argue with me. But my next statement is far from self-evident. At first blush, in fact, it will sound crazy to many readers and negotiators:

The wise negotiator knows that
only one person in a negotiation absolutely
must feel okay. That person is *not you*.

Some people are baffled initially by this lesson, if not positively antagonistic. The lesson is correct, however. If it was good enough for Abraham Lincoln in his negotiation with his constituents and army, it is good enough for you. As Lincoln understood, being un-okay is extraordinarily effective as a tool in a negotiation. By letting *the other person* be a little more okay, you start to bring down barriers. By allowing him or her to feel okay, you, like Lincoln, like Columbo, are actually in control.

Lincoln's behavior was both calculated and heartfelt. He really did connect with the common folks. Today, he'd probably be advised to hire experts to dress him in styles and colors that would compensate for his gaunt physique. What did Lincoln himself do? He actually *accentuated* his harsh looks. His signature stovepipe hat made him 7 feet tall. His pants were always too short, accentuating his long legs. He always wore black, which accentuates thinness (or so I'm told). He usually rode a horse so small that any stirrups long enough for his legs practically dragged on the ground. He looked ridiculous sitting on a horse. And this was all carefully calculated to help him come across as a common man, as Uncle Abe, as someone his constituents could trust.

Ronald Reagan, intentionally or unintentionally, was a master at appearing less than okay at press conferences. He would stammer around and laugh at himself before he answered a question, and then his answer might not have been much of one at all. But he was effective in the end, wasn't he? Winston Churchill was an unprepossessing butterball who wanted to be photographed with his even more unprepossessing bulldog. Surely you've noticed how effective keynote and after-dinner speakers tell a self-deprecating story in the first few minutes of their performances. Their first implicit message to the audience is this: You may be paying me $20,000 to stand up here, and my suit may be more expensive than yours, but I'm no better than you. I'm just folks, too. And this is not gamesmanship on the speaker's part. This is *honesty*, because, in the final analysis, everyone on this planet is just folks, one of the gang—a big gang, to be sure, but just a gang. We're all in this boat together. We're all human. We've all made a mistake today and we'll make another one tomorrow, very possibly a whopper. People who pretend otherwise fool no one but themselves (if they really fool themselves).

As a negotiator, you must take the same approach. If you can emulate Lincoln and Reagan and, yes, even Columbo to some small degree, if you can be not quite okay in your own way, you will exponentially increase your negotiating success.

Ralph Waldo Emerson wrote in his profound essay "On Compensation," "Our greatest strength is our greatest weakness." How true. We tend to overplay our hand, so to speak, but as negotiators we must control this instinct while welcoming it from everyone else. If the other party likes to show off his glibness, let him, and pay very close attention while you're at it, because his lack of restraint might well lead him to give up much more information than he should. If he can't resist the opportunity to play to his charm, let him. If she likes to demonstrate her extraordinary grasp of the finest points of maritime law, let her. The trained negotiator is more than happy to let everyone show off in almost any way, because that greatest strength may eventually become the greatest weakness.

Recall the story about the company losing money on every shipment. If it had continued to ship its product at the contracted price with its primary customer, it would have gone out of business. Renegotiation of contracts was mandatory. But no one in the organization thought this was even possible. They thought this move would look "unprofessional." They said, "We're going to look like fools." The president balked as well, until I finally got his attention by asking, "How long do you want to continue to tape a $100,000 check to the side of each machine?"

Remember what the president said when he called his counterpart with another company: "We did a terrible job negotiating with you. You probably knew that at the time. I didn't. Now I do. How can we fix this?" This was the truth. It needed to be said. It was an excellent way to say "No, we can't continue with this contract," but it was also effective as a way to be un-okay. This admission helped to disarm the other executive. Nor was it unprofessional to make such an admission.

You're going to run into abusive people in negotiations. Some are trained to deliberately behave in an abusive manner and some are just not nice people. Whatever the motivation, you can't allow their behavior to drive yours. They may call you names and accuse you of unprofessional behavior. What should you do? Do you get needy and then defensive and then aggressive and fight back against this behavior? No. You listen calmly and show no neediness whatsoever. Let's take a look at an example. Jeff is a purchasing representative of a very large pharmaceutical company and is trained to be abusive. Susan is a representative of a global chemical company who sells to Jeff. They meet at Jeff's office and Jeff begins with, "Well, Susan, I am going to cut right to the chase. Your arrogance is going to cost you this account. Time and again we have requested discounts from you and you have rejected each request out of your arrogance over this contract. You know we have needed your chemicals and you have held our feet to the fire. This is going to stop. You are not a good partner and you're not someone we can count on to help us. Your arrogance is going to cause you to lose this account."

Well, what does Susan say? I hope something like "Jeff, you probably should fire us. I don't see how this can ever be fixed. I am stuck. It's out of my hands. The problem is until this contract is completed, which is not for another ninety days. I can't open discussions on the existing contract. I can begin discussions on a new contract. What would you like me to do?"

The discussion continues:

> "You don't get it Susan. If you don't discount the current contract, there will be no discussion on a new contract. You guys are out. Period. You go tell your boss that."

"Jeff, it's worse than that. If I even bring up the existing contract to my boss, I won't be back to see you except to ask you for a job. But, seriously, how much risk do you want to take with that foreign supplier?"

"Risk, what do you mean?"

"Well, here's the problem: We have bailed out three other customers when shipments didn't arrive on time. How much risk do you want to take with their being late?"

Let me repeat that point: I am *not* suggesting that you appear unprofessional. I'm simply asking you not to be afraid of honesty—not to be afraid of being less than perfect. Do you enjoy being around the perfect person? Most of us don't. People want to deal with a regular person. In a negotiation, being less okay is just showing a foible now and then. Struggle a little. Borrow a pen or paper to take notes. Search for the right words to ask questions. Letting other people help you is an excellent way to help them feel more okay. It also says to them, "What you see is what you get."

I often suggest to people I coach that they leave their briefcase or business cards at home for the first meeting. Maybe you just won't do such a thing, but I'm here to tell you that this lack of perfection or something similar can be so powerful it's scary. I once coached a law professor—call him Lawrence—who believed he always had to be perfect. Funniest thing: Lawrence had trouble getting people to share their most important thoughts. I asked him to try something for me. In the next discussion he led, he was to remove his suit jacket, loosen his tie, and roll up his sleeves, or at least flip their cuffs up. And I suggested that should the discussion become a little heated by emotion, he should step back two steps and "reduce" his presence. Not long after that coaching session, I got a call from Japan very early one morning. It was Lawrence, who had just completed the greatest meeting of his career. This Japanese group wanted to contract with him to lead discussions at their university for the next year for a handsome honorarium.

Perhaps you want to call this gamesmanship, but I disagree. The professor didn't get the contract because he loosened his tie. He got the contract because the audience was comfortable and felt safe and okay with his humanity. This is not trivial gamesmanship. This is honesty, the honesty of being a little less than okay, which breaks down barriers.

The tougher the negotiation, the more critical it is to understand that if someone in the room has to feel okay, it is *not* you. If someone has to feel not-okay, it *is* you.

When other people don't feel okay, they set up barriers much faster than you can break them down. But "not-okayness" on your part breaks down their barriers—like magic, often.

This behavior is easier said than done, I realize, because from the day we're born we're fighting for our okayness, and then we're almost *trained* to fight for it. And of course we see pictures of the titans of industry—maybe the CEO of the very company we work for—dressed to the nines as they savor their power breakfasts, power lunches, power dinners, power aperitifs, and power cigars. These people are okay beyond belief. I think of Meryl Streep in *The Devil Wears Prada* as she walks in the door and throws her fur onto the desk without as much as a good morning, or her superior attitude as she deals with the employees who are terrified if she walks down the hallway in their general direction. Such tycoons' lives and incredible okayness are what we're supposed to want and *need*. And here I am suggesting that you get to the top by presenting yourself as less okay!

In the context of a negotiation, yes, I am. I'm not saying you show up with a stain on your shirt or blouse. Just a little something that's less than perfect to inject a little humanity, a little vulnerability. If you're fortunate, like former Presidents Gerald Ford and Bill Clinton (a bipartisan illustration), you have a natural talent for making people feel okay. President Ford was always seen as the scholar athlete from down the street whom everyone could talk to. He had no enemies. President Clinton was a master of the look-down smile with a chuckle or laugh that put the audience at ease. He does have enemies, but even they admit that he can connect with anyone, given the one-on-one opportunity. But if you're not so fortunate as those two presidents, you'll have to work a little harder, and if you have to be not-okay in order to do so, then so be it. (And some people, let's face it, just have the unfortunate knack of making those around them feel not okay. I don't recommend professional negotiation as a career choice for these folks.)

If you have any doubts about the wisdom of the advice in this chapter, it couldn't be easier to check out.

Test Drive The next time you find yourself in a situation in which the other party is maybe just a little standoffish or doubtful, try being a little less okay. Pretend your pen has run out of ink and ask to borrow one for a moment. Or search your pocket for your notepad and come up short and ask to borrow a slip of paper. Or pretend the battery of your Palm Pilot has run out of power—again. And then try to tell me you don't notice an immediate, beneficial difference in the atmosphere of this "negotiation."

Three-Minute Checklist

- Stop, look, listen. What are your temptations to feel needy in this situation? Simply identifying them helps you control them.
- Likewise, how are you tempted to be okay at the expense of the other side? Simple identification helps you check that okayness.
- What are *their* temptations to neediness? To be okay?

Encourage them in these regards. Their neediness is to your advantage.

If you find yourself thinking about what you can give up in order to get this agreement, stop. Some neediness of some kind is showing. Go back to the first item in this checklist.

2

So You Want Results?

Focus on What You Can Control—Yourself

Can home-run hitters control the results of their mighty swings? No. Some pitches are almost literally unhittable, or the outfielder may climb the wall and make the catch, or a jet stream may keep the ball in the park. All the slugger can do is work hard in practice on his mechanics and try to put a pure swing on the ball during the game. He thinks only in terms of executing his mechanics and maintaining his power and leverage. If he thinks in terms of *homers,* he loses power and leverage by overswinging and lunging at bad pitches.

Or golf. Instead of having a goal of breaking par (or bogey, more likely, for the amateur), a result you cannot control, you should concentrate on putting your best swing on the ball, an action you can control. You should also concentrate on a sound plan of "course management," as the pros say. This you can also control. For average golfers, course management often boils down to not trying shots way beyond their talents—shots they never practice. Instead, make effective decisions and say no to your ego.

The distinction is crystal-clear, but some people who nod their heads in agreement with these simple sports analogies will turn right around and announce that their goal in their business is to close the deal by a certain date or sell a specified number of widgets in a specified amount of time. In fact, this is conventional wisdom in the business world. Such wisdom tells you to set long-term goals, overall goals, written goals, big goals, pie-in-the-sky goals. But do you really have control over these kinds of performance goals? I'm afraid not. These are *results* over which you have no more control than the slugger has over his home-run total for the year. But many companies and professionals set them anyway. I have worked for years with men and women who may earn in the high six figures in commissions, with top executives of Fortune 500 companies, and with college graduates preparing for their first real job. Invariably, all of these good people tell me they want the same thing. Results!

I now ask you to take a very different approach, one that will change your life. If you want to be a successful negotiator in any field—the most successful salesperson you can be—you must *not* set quantitative targets, quotas, numbers, or percentages. No such "performance goals" whatsoever. None of that. Never! Those are results over which you have absolutely no final control.

What can you truly control? Only your actions and your behavior. What you say, how you say it, your use of time, your preparation, your mission and purpose—all subjects of upcoming chapters. You cannot control the *other party's* actions and decisions, not directly, but you can control your assessment of those actions and decisions, and, with practice, you can definitely control your own actions and decisions and behavior, and you can keep your emotions, including your neediness, under check. You cannot control your anger following an insult—the emotion itself—but you can control what you do with that anger. You do decide whether to strike back in some way or to turn the other cheek.

In your life and negotiations, you develop habits of behavior, good and bad, and you have activities that you pursue

that help or hinder you. Any negotiator ⸺
this point is way, way ahead of most ⸺
"professional" negotiators. Goals to in⸺
behavior are the only valid goals, be⸺
ones you can control, and achieving⸺
through any negotiation and lead to all u⸺
But concentrating on the numerical results as your goal is a ⸺
rible waste of time and energy.

Think behavior. Forget results.

In the preceding chapter, about the dangers of neediness, I introduced my rule *No closing,* because the rush to close betrays neediness and therefore puts the other party on instant red alert, as well it should. This *No closing* rule also applies in spades in this chapter about the folly of chasing results, because the rush to close is the epitome of chasing results you cannot actually control. Yet many people in sales, especially, are subjected to bosses urging them, in one way or another, to "close, close, close."

What if one of these bosses happens to be your boss? You can't just ignore her. How do you proceed? I suggest you use the new system of negotiation learned from this book to help this boss discover what you have discovered. That is, *negotiate* with her. Give her this book. Lay out the principles. Ask for her rebuttal. Ask for the opportunity to demonstrate what you have learned.

No luck? This person will never listen or never learn? You should think seriously about a new venue for your labors, because at this one you're going to have a hard time overcoming the obstacles and fulfilling your potential. The fact that you're reading this book, looking for help, almost says as much.

Now let's consider the following test drive for the *No closing* rule, the ultimate way to avoid chasing results and neediness. Told about this test, people have said to me, "You're kidding,

ot at all. In fact, there's no big risk here—not really.
may seem ridiculously contrarian at first sight is just
mmon sense.

Test Drive If you work in sales and the customer is
ready to pick up the pen and sign this modest contract, try saying (and *meaning*), "This is wonderful, Mrs. Johnson, but I want
you to be positive this is the right decision for you. Let's go
through it again. Let's be sure." Does this invitation give Mrs.
Johnson more confidence or less confidence in the deal she's
about to sign? More confidence—in *you*. Her degree of conviction goes *up*, for the simple reason that you, the salesperson,
are confident that the agreement will survive further consideration. Your confidence feeds her confidence. You're not trying
to rush her and you're not trying to close her. In direct sales,
there's another side to enhanced satisfaction on the buyer's
part: referrals. But don't take my word for it. With a modest contract, give it a shot—a test drive.

WITH QUOTAS, FAILURE IS FAILURE, AND SUCCESS IS ALSO FAILURE

I have seen many businesspeople banging their heads against
quotas they have no chance of meeting. The boss thinks this ar-
tificial number spurs them on, and maybe it does, but it spurs
them on to do what, exactly? One clever version of the answer
was provided a couple of years ago by Hall of Fame basketball
center Bill Walton when told that Shaquille O'Neal, a bad free-
throw shooter, had been practicing hard in recent months.
"Okay," Walton quipped, in almost so many words, "but is he
just practicing his mistakes?" If the ball goes in for Shaq, it's
mainly luck; you don't even have to know basketball to see
that clearly. His mechanics at the free-throw line are terrible.

As I put it, Shaq was working *harder,* not *smarter.* That's what
happens in the business world when the boss spurs the team

on to meet an elusive quota of some sort. The pressure mounts every day. Instead of concentrating on their own actions, in all likelihood the team just hustles, sweats, flails around, makes a million phone calls, begs people to sign, and maybe even threatens people if they don't sign. What a vicious circle: chasing a number; working *harder,* not *smarter;* developing bad habits; and digging a deeper and deeper hole.

And then what happens? If at all possible, compromise. Say anything and accept anything, just get that signature! Of course, this is the classic mistake of win-win thinking, an unnecessary compromise brought on by neediness and chasing results. But there is another way. Consider my client Brian, many of whose customers waited until the very end of the quarter before placing their orders. Their thinking was simple: Maybe Brian would have to compromise on the price or some other aspect of the negotiation in order to meet his *numbers*—ultimately his company's numbers, but by extension, the numbers Wall Street was waiting for. This classic win-win tactic works a million times a day around the world, but it doesn't work with Brian. He doesn't chase numbers. His mission and purpose won't let him. He works hard, yes, but he also works smart. He stays within his system.

Chasing a performance goal over which you have no final control is a tragic waste of talent and energy. What's more, a numerical quota you *do* meet is *still* a counterproductive, dangerous goal. My first lesson here came when I was thirteen years old and selling Cokes at the Fairgrounds Coliseum during the high school basketball playoffs. We kids would net a nickel per cup sold. I decided that two bucks for the night would be a handsome profit, so I set a goal for myself of forty Cokes. If I reached it, I would relax and watch the rest of the triple-header. Well, I hustled up and down the aisles, yelling, "Ice-cold Coke! Coke right here!" But the beverage practically sold itself. I hit my number in the first half of the first game, cashed in, found a seat in the back row, and started cheering. The next day at school I ran into my chum Gary Huston, who had also been selling Cokes at the games, and I smugly asked him how much money he'd made. He said, "Well, I want a new tire for my motor scooter, which costs six dollars, so I decided to work until the last buzzer sounded in the third game and then counted my nickels. I made twenty-four dollars."

I was shocked. That was a long time ago and an important lesson learned. Little did I know that adults—professionals— are making the same mistake I did. They've met their number and it's only Wednesday! *Man, I'm great. I'll relax the rest of the week. It's my reward.* Fine—for those who want to settle for less than their best. Such folks are not achieving anything close to what they could achieve, all because their goals are invalid, while the Brians and the Gary Hustons of the world are succeeding at the highest levels because they set goals over which they have complete control: their activities and behaviors.

BEWARE UNWORTHY ACTIVITY GOALS

Setting unmanageable goals and chasing results beyond your control is one common mistake. Another is wasting time and energy on activity goals that *are* manageable but not nearly the best way to spend your time. I hereby draw a distinction between what I call *payside* and *nonpayside* activities. Payside is everything directly related to a specific negotiation. Nonpayside is stuff you have to do, but it isn't directly on the track of a specific negotiation. For example, filling out expense forms and other sorts of bureaucratic paperwork: These are, clearly, the most menial forms of nonpayside activity. You may have to do them, but don't let them become an end in themselves. I've seen it happen many times: The desktop is perfectly neat, the files beautifully organized, everything is shipshape, the office manager loves you, but where are the actual negotiations, much less the agreements and the deals and the sales? Some nonpay activity is necessary in order to get to payside, but you must keep it to a minimum. Most of all, you don't want to confuse the importance of the two.

For the salesperson, lining up appointments with truly qualified prospects is definitely payside activity—no appointments, no sales, by definition—but rustling up almost certainly worthless appointments from the phone book, merely for the sake of fulfilling some mandatory quota, is *not* payside activity. As I mentioned earlier, cold-calling is an excellent training ground, and when valid appointments result it is a valuable activity. But *begging* for an appointment is an extremely common error in all fields of business. I have seen salespeople almost ruined by this kind of nonpayside *dreaming*. This begged appointment will probably fail, and so will the next one like it, and pretty soon, no matter how strong they are, these people's self-image will suffer, their neediness will soar, and then they're really in trouble. I've written earlier about the salutary discipline imposed by cold-calling, but make no mistake: It is nonpayside activity. Be sure you understand this.

When I first started out selling water softeners to supplement my income as a pilot, I worked for a man who saddled me with a performance goal of five presentations a day to anyone who would listen. I did that. I begged for the time for my demonstration. A few people said okay, show me this thing, but most said no. Even from the actual demonstrations I got no buyers. The best I got was "You'll have to talk to my husband" or "You'll have to talk to my wife." At the end of one demonstration I found out I'd been dealing with the babysitter. Oh boy. That's about when the light started to come on in my head, when I realized I was completely stuck in the worst kind of nonpay activity. What a waste of time. I realized I had to find out who made the decisions in a given household. I wasn't thinking in payside and nonpayside terms at the time, not specifically, but the difference was forming in my mind. I would demonstrate the water softener only for actual decision-makers who could write the check. That's great payside activity, *even if they said, "No, thanks."* I wanted to hear yes, of course, but no was just fine. This demonstration had not been a waste of time. It was payside work.

You must be aware of the difference between dealing with people who can actually make decisions and dealing with the babysitters, and every company I've ever encountered has lots of babysitters, people who may even pretend they can make the decisions but really can't. I discuss this surprisingly important subject in more detail in Chapter 9. My point here is that only work that drives the decision with real decision-makers is payside activity. Say you have a meeting with the production team committee of a company to which your company is about to submit a proposal. You get the details you need to complete the proposal and leave all charged up because you got the information and got along great with the committee. They seemed to really like you. You think you have the inside track and you return to your team and report how great the meeting was. But that meeting was really just about filling squares for the committee and other meaningless paperwork, and the production team manager on the committee is unlikely to be the sole decision-maker for the other company. That meeting was nonpayside. Go, get the information, get along with the committee, gather important information, but don't mistake the meeting as the great advantage provider in the negotiation process. It's not.

Consider the job search of a woman I'll call Linda, a friend of my daughter's. Linda had just finished college and was working part-time as a waitress while searching for a job in her field of marketing. In her spare time, Linda spent many hours scouring the Web for job openings and filling out online applications. She followed up with phone calls to the Human Resources people to make sure she was following the correct procedures. After three months, Linda had not received one interview. Why? She was definitely working hard, but it was all nonpayside activity, because she was not reaching the people who actually made the hiring decisions.

I watched Linda's campaign from afar, getting reports from

my daughter, until I finally couldn't take it anymore and asked my young friend if she'd be interested in some help. If so, was she ready to try *whatever I suggested?* Yes, she said, and I had a new *pro bono* client. First, I instructed Linda make a list of the places she really wanted to work. I then asked her to call the assistant to the CEO or president of each of these companies and ask this assistant, "How do I meet your CEO/president? I would like the opportunity to discuss with him/her a future career with your company. When could I do that?"

This was cold calling and therefore nonpayside activity, but it had some value because at least she was talking with an individual who could introduce her to a decision-maker. There were fourteen companies on Linda's list. She got four appointments with a decision-maker, seven references to the HR people, and three directions to the website. The two of us prepared for the actual appointments with decision-makers and the less-valuable appointments with the HR people. She rejected the website companies. Within three weeks, Linda was hired by one of the companies on her list, and as I write, she is finishing her training in Paris.

A particularly dicey issue with payside versus nonpayside activity is wining and dining and golfing. In some fields, such expense account entertainment is expected, and if you're dining with a decision-maker, this may well be payside activity. It may be great payside activity, but I've seen extremely competent people fall into the trap of believing that all their meals and all their rounds of golf were productive payside activity, and they weren't. It was all very seductive, but where was the serious negotiating? How did these activities move the negotiation forward? This is pretty common, actually, throughout the business world, as well as in the more one-on-one professions, including straight sales. These folks either don't know the difference between payside and nonpayside activity or—the critical point here—they do know the difference but are using all this nonpayside wining and dining to avoid what they know will be the difficult nuts and bolts of the negotiation.

You see, with nonpayside activity, there's no immediate gain, but neither is there immediate *risk:* no need to say no, no need to hear no, no need to exercise discipline, no need to watch out for neediness, and no reason to make disciplined decisions of any kind, because you're really not negotiating yet. Such pretending and stalling tempt all of us at times, and succumbing now and then won't be the end of our world. But when they become a habit—and they can, very easily—well, this is very dangerous when you're trying to make a living. You must develop the discipline that allows you to be able and willing to set aside any nonpayside work—even a round of golf at a favorite club—relating to any negotiation, even a very large one, in favor of true payside activity on a much smaller negotiation. One of the characteristics of really successful negotiators is how swiftly and efficiently they shift from nonpayside activity to payside activity when the opportunity presents itself. I know extremely disciplined (and therefore successful) people who would not think twice about canceling a ceremonial round at Pebble Beach with non-decision-makers for a major client—great fun, but nonpayside—in favor of a final meeting with a potential customer perhaps ready to open only a modest account. I also know very successful people who would cancel the latter meeting and play the ceremonial golf instead. Fine, I won't criticize that decision, but I would bet that they had all the bases covered and knew not to show need.

When you have the habit of setting as a goal *only* activity that you can accomplish and that is genuinely productive, you've taken an enormous step in your career. Rather than succeeding or not succeeding almost by accident in the service of some result that's really beyond your control, you're taking responsibility for your actions and ending what might be self-deception (and probably company-wide deception). This may sound harsh, but it's the truth. In a way, it's relatively easy to sell or not sell fifty widgets this week, or to sign or fail to sign the contract with your supplier. It's relatively easy to keep massaging a potential customer and easy to schedule another round of saying and hearing maybe. It is more challenging to proceed in a disciplined, systematic way. It is more challenging to control neediness and to say and hear no. But this is what you must do in order to achieve what you're capable of.

Beware the seductions of nonpayside activity.

THE NEGOTIATION NEVER ENDS

Weak conventional wisdom holds that the negotiation ends when the deal is put to bed—when the paper is signed, before the ink has even dried. But if this were true, we would never encounter lawsuits, canceled pay raises, renegotiated contracts, or "buyer's remorse." We wouldn't need lawyers (or as many lawyers). Customers wouldn't change suppliers, and suppliers wouldn't decide they don't want anything to do with some customers again. The homeowner wouldn't have to call the pool contractor for touch-up work. The parents wouldn't have to call the teacher for a follow-up session. In the real world, the negotiation does *not* end when the papers are signed. In fact, tough corporate negotiators work under the *presumption* that contracts are easily broken, that this is just part of business. After all, Fortune 500 corporations have more legal staying power than the smaller businesses they're dealing with. Heck, Microsoft has more staying power than the federal government, and that's the truth. There are even corporations out there that place orders with small suppliers with no intention of paying for at least six months. They promise 30 days, but so what? This promise means nothing to them, but what it should mean to the small supplier is to be ready for further negotiation, regardless of what the contract says.

So when does a negotiation *really* end? Take a minute to think back on some of the most critical negotiations in your business or private life. Did they really end, or did they keep going? Some of them kept going, I know that. Negotiations with kids—teenagers, specifically—are the classic example. Most of them never end. That's a given. In the business world, this takes the form of the late payment, the late delivery, the new question about the clause on page 17, the request for a small favor now that the deal is signed—there are thousands of such tactics. The important question is how you react to these provocations. If your invalid goal had been "to sign the agreement and collect the money," chances are you're upset about the late payment or the delay in delivery or the quibble about the boilerplate clause. Maybe this new development makes you think you were taken advantage of in the original deal. In any event, you probably don't know what to do next. You made the mistake of thinking the negotiation was over. Now it turns out not to be over, and you have no idea what to do next. But if your valid goal in the negotiation all along had not been to sign and collect but to manage your behavior and your activity while executing your system, you have no problem at all with these latest developments. You build plans for the next, the next, and so on. Back to work! No big deal.

BREAKING BAD HABITS

Mike is a successful financial planner with a focused niche market: doctors. Mike and his team had a tremendous work ethic. He was often invited to speak to medical groups all over the state, which was quite a platform. His company was successful, no doubt about it, but he had reached a plateau. Why had Mike's business stopped growing? When he started analyzing every aspect of his work, he realized that he was leaving long-winded messages and leaving multiple messages without waiting for a return call. He found himself *telling* instead of *asking* and *listening* (the subject of an upcoming chapter). He realized he was out there trying to drum up speaking engagements instead of waiting calmly to be invited. He was taking any appointment he could get. In short, he had slipped into a neediness mode, and the doctors could sense this. Because of this neediness, he was chasing results—not a numerical quota, exactly, but results over which he had no final control. He was working harder, not smarter. And the bad habits he was falling into were getting in the way of his company's success.

Breaking old, weak, or bad habits and replacing them with new, more effective habits is always a challenge. How many New Year's resolutions really succeed? Without a lot of discipline, very few.

So how do you find the discipline to change poor negotiating habits? How do you let go of numbers? How do you refrain from rushing to close deals? How do you forget results you can't control in the end anyway? You build the activity and behavior habits over which you maintain self-control. You monitor yourself and your behavior daily, and you do this as rigorously as fighter pilots. You may think this is a far-fetched analogy, but stay with me, if you will.

One of the most challenging skills anyone can learn is flying ultrasophisticated military jets. The oxygen mask and parachute alone are very restrictive and are smothering enough to make you want to vomit. Sitting in a cockpit so small and with straps so tight you can barely move or turn your shoulders is also stifling. It's not a joy ride at an amusement park. Speeds of 700 miles per hour require quick, effective decision-making. There is no doubt that death can be instantaneous if the wrong decisions are made, so it is a gross understatement to say a young pilot faces a tremendous challenge. How does the military, in 12 short months, turn a young college graduate into a superb pilot? How does this pilot build the activity and behavior habits necessary to fly this incredible machine? The process starts very simply. The student pilots are issued a daily training folder in which they record everything. That record is carried at all times and reviewed by the instructor and the flight leader—reviewed two or three times a day, in fact, with constant emphasis on reward for success and focused hard work on the failures.

How do you, as a student of negotiation, turn newly learned activity and behavior into habit? You, too, should keep a daily record and use it to identify strengths and weaknesses. Though I'm not a psychologist and this is not a book about psychology, I do ask you, the negotiator, to take into account human nature. You must understand and engage the folks with whom you're negotiating as psychological beings, and you must engage *yourself* in the same way. This daily habit of analyzing your own actions and correcting them when necessary is critical to success. It's something that many of us do at least some of the time—sometimes explicitly—and in my hands-on work as teacher and coach, I ask my students to make a commitment to daily, active self-examination and assessment and to monitor their behavior and emotions as they affect the negotiating process. Vince Lombardi said that "winning isn't everything, but the will to prepare to win *is* everything."

When Mike, the financial planner who had let bad habits creep in, tracked his daily activity, he quickly saw the problem. Instead of leaving needy messages, he simply asked his clients to call him. He now waited a few days for the return calls, which did come. He learned to structure questions and create vision instead of telling and creating objections. He canceled a speaking engagement and rescheduled it. Now Mike makes himself available to the medical community as a valuable resource, but he no longer chases anyone. Mike uses a checklist with each potential client, and no potential client ever feels the full-court press coming, because there is no full-court press. There is only Mike's knowledge and experience. Mike has left the plateau so far behind he can't even see it in the rearview mirror.

For many people, keeping track of their daily activity is a difficult task. But I also know that keeping track will be as valuable in your negotiating work as anything else you might do. The critical assessment pinpoints weaknesses, works with strengths, and develops self-esteem. This discipline makes you really stop to think how you're spending your time, how you're seeing and correcting mistakes, how you're progressing as a negotiator. It helps you see clearly what you can and cannot control.

Some theories of learning suggest that we humans need 800 hours of practice to learn something new and complex. Maybe that's high for some tasks, I don't know, but I do know that we need lots of practice. Keeping track helps you get it. Just set activity goals and behavior goals every day. At the end of the day, take a moment to reflect on how you did. You'll be surprised. I urge you to make this commitment to yourself.

Three-Minute Checklist

- Are you playing a "numbers" game, even a subtle one? It's just a cop-out. Focus instead on your activity and behavior.
- The temptation to "close" is powerful and in some businesses, like real estate, almost ingrained. You must keep a sharp eye. Are you subtly trying to "close" this agreement?
- Hold everything. Is this phone call or this meeting payside or nonpayside? Are you kidding yourself about its value?
- Did you start setting and evaluating activity and behavior goals daily?

3

If You Want the Advantage, Take "No" for the Answer

Why "No" Is Great, "Yes" Is Bad, and "Maybe" Is the Worst

When I first started working as a commercial airline pilot thirty-five years ago, my salary was not enough to make ends meet for my family, so I dabbled in a couple of other business ventures. Since my flying took me to the Far East, one of those ventures was an attempt to start an import company that specialized in ship artifacts available from suppliers in Hong Kong. On one of my many 20-hour flights to Hong Kong, I read a book on negotiation, expecting help in my new business venture. This book thoroughly indoctrinated me with the idea that everyone is supposed to give up something for the sake of the deal: What's good for me is good for you. This made sense to me, but when I started trying to make deals for the artifacts, I quickly realized that the folks on the other side of the table hadn't read the same book and certainly didn't have my interests in mind at all. They didn't seem to care whether I succeeded or not. They weren't open to giving discounts based on the promised future business I would bring, and they certainly weren't willing to give up something for the good of the deal. "No can do" was their answer to just about every offer I put on the table.

What was going on here? Why wasn't "what's good for me is good for you" getting me to "yes"? After all, my rules were the ones propagated by business schools and taken to heart by an untold number of negotiators in this country. My rules were grounded in the idea that a negotiation takes into account the "legitimate interests" of each side, resolves conflict "fairly," is "durable," and considers overall "community interests." This had all sounded pretty good to me—until I stepped into the real world of these ship artifact dealers in Hong Kong, who were negotiating by a completely different set of rules from the ones I'd learned from the negotiation book.

That experience made me think more carefully about the idea of negotiation set forth in that book. I realized that the nice words about legitimate interests and community interests and fairness sound great, but like too many politicians' poll-driven speeches, that's as far as they go. They sound good. The intellectual content is minimal. Exactly who decides which interests in the negotiation are "legitimate"? What authority bestows this blessing? Does a "durable" agreement need to last a month, a year, a decade, or a lifetime? (If you ask the owner of a Viper automobile how durable the tires are, she'll give you the answer in miles. If you ask the owner of a bicycle the same question, he'll answer in terms of time.) And how about those community interests? There certainly are many of them. Off the top, I can start with schools, employee groups, entrepreneurial developers, taxpayers, the environment, and the city hall bureaucracy. These interests are often in conflict. Which ones should a particular negotiation take into account? Who decides?

Think carefully about the standard definition of a wise agreement and you start getting a bit frustrated. How do the business schools and academia get away with this stuff? It's absolutely meaningless! What's "legitimate" is all in the eye of the beholder. Likewise with "fairness," with "durable," with "community interest." In Hong Kong, I learned this lesson well. I was completely frustrated by my inability to get anywhere with the suppliers. One day, finished with my futile efforts and with a little time to kill before my flight back to New York City via Anchorage, I stopped by a bookstore near the Peninsula Hotel in Hong Kong and found myself in front of the *Oxford English Dictionary*. Out of idle curiosity, I looked up "negotiation." And there it was:

> A negotiation is the effort to bring about an agreement between two or more parties, with all parties having the RIGHT to VETO.

Eureka! These words struck me like a bolt of lightning. All these many years later I remember the moment clearly. A negotiation is simply the effort to bring about agreement between two or more parties, with all parties having the right to veto. Now, the right to veto is the right to say no, isn't it? Indeed it is. Nothing more, nothing less, nothing fancy, nothing meaningless.

The definition of negotiation contained no meaningless passages about fairness and legitimacy. Instead, just that one word, "no." If you don't like what's happening in the negotiation, say no and we'll go from there. If I don't like what's happening, I'll say no and we'll go from there.

I've previously mentioned that my early attempts to bolster my flying income consisted of selling water-softening systems. I was working hard and following the company's sales techniques. I was good at proclaiming the many benefits of water softeners, I gave a pretty good demo for anyone who would pretend to pay attention, and I never forgot to ask for the order. I was good at hearing "maybe call back next month," but I made very few actual sales. Returning from that particular trip to Hong Kong, I decided I had very little to lose by trying a negotiation based on the simple principle as stated in the dictionary—that any sale, any negotiation, is rooted in the right to veto. At my first opportunity I returned to one of my first contacts, the Dixon home, knocked on the door, reintroduced myself to the lady of the house, and said, "Mrs. Dixon, I don't know if you remember, but I'm Jim Camp and I represent Goleta Water Softeners. The last time I was here you told me you were tired of hard water, but somehow I goofed up that sale. I just want to ask you to go ahead and tell me 'No, thanks,' if that's your decision, so I can move on and close the file."

Then the strangest thing happened. Mrs. Dixon said, "You didn't goof up. I just couldn't afford the system last month, but now I want to buy it. Can you install it this month?"

I could and I did. I soon returned to the home of every single person I had seen in recent weeks, thirty-one in total. I asked each of them to just tell me no if they weren't interested in the softening system. I would close their file and be no further bother to them. I sold six systems. Within months I was making more money selling water-softening systems than I was flying big jet airplanes. There was no doubt that a major reason was my invitation to my potential customers to tell me no.

RESISTANCE TO "NO"

This use of "no" seems uncontroversial enough, and it is, but when I describe this key principle of my negotiation system, well, it's the one idea that hard-charging businesspeople, specifically, find the hardest to truly accept and then put into practice. At the beginning of training sessions, I ask what "no" means to them. It means the end, they say. It means good-bye, walk away, never return, total rejection, it's all over, I have failed, and so on. When people finally get their minds around the concept and master the use of "no," it's a different story. When you internalize the principle that in every negotiation every party has the right to say no, that "no" is just a decision

that may be followed by another decision, and that it is a perfectly *safe* answer to give and to hear, well, the results are magical. But I don't want to kid you. It's not always a smooth ride.

So what causes the resistance? Let's go way back for a moment to your Terrible Twos, when you discover this incredible
word. The declaration *"No!"* gives you—for the first time in
your young life—a little empowerment, but it also comes with
the downside of conflict with your parents, because "no" is
a two-way street. You carry this experience with you the rest
of your life. The mindset is cast in concrete: "No" is a dangerous word.

> Everyone wants to be liked, and if you say no you'll be
> disliked.

> You don't want to hurt someone's feelings, and if you say no
> you'll hurt his feelings or, worse, you might damage his ego
> beyond all repair. Then what have you done? You surely can't
> recover from that mistake.

> You don't want to come across as too blunt or surly or arro-
> gant or demanding, and if you say no you come off as all that
> and more. In your heart, however, you know you are not a
> mean person.

> When you say no, you're walking away. When you hear no,
> they are walking away, because "no" is final—"no" is the end.
> It's over. It's a defeat.

> You would rather die than "lose," and if they say no you lose.

> "No" is failure, and failure is just not acceptable in my family.
> How about yours?

> What do you mean they told you no? You're not a loser!
> You're a winner! Never let anyone tell you no again!

This is the win-win mindset, of course, which teaches that
the word we want is *yes!* This mindset is compromise- and fear-
based. It's nothing but emotions, and we are so immersed in

this atmosphere that saying no just sounds too harsh. Not too long ago a friend happened to catch and report to me on a segment of the *Today Show* on NBC about "the art of saying no." This discussion wasn't about negotiation, specifically, just about "no" in general and our cultural unwillingness to say it even when we should. "No" is to be avoided like the plague, while "yes" is the acceptance of all things we think and do and are. It's the American way of life!

I intend to convince you otherwise.

> **"No," the word you have been trained to fear, is, in fact, the word that will change your life for the better, forever.**

MAYBE SO, MAYBE NOT

We're afraid to say no, so what do we say instead? Often, we say maybe. "Maybe" won't hurt their feelings. "Maybe" won't reject them. "Maybe" won't kill the deal. No losers with "maybe"! But where does "maybe" get you in a negotiation? Absolutely nowhere. With "maybe," neither party has any idea where things stand. If you say maybe, you haven't said enough to elicit a useful response or information from the other side because you haven't really said anything at all. It definitely does not give either side anything to work with. You've muddied the waters— nothing more. And when you *hear* maybe, your emotions are all over the place.

> "Hey Dad, can I use the car Friday for the dance?"
> "*Another* dance? Well, we'll see. I'll think about it."
> "Okay, Dad. Thanks."

This scenario dates me, I understand. It sounds a little quaint for the twenty-first century, but the point here is valid. What's this teenager thinking? "Well, Dad didn't say no. I guess it's looking good so far." And what is Dad thinking? "Gee, I don't know about this. I'm just not comfortable with his driving a bunch of kids around. I'd better get my wife on my side before I tell him no, or if she feels strongly enough about his going, I'll have to say yes. Let's just see what happens. Maybe this will go away on its own."

It won't go away on its own. The "maybe" bought Dad a little time, that's all. In the family setting, okay, buy some time, but in the business world, this time bought is time *lost*. The buyer wants a discount; the seller says maybe. The seller wants a larger order to justify a discount; the buyer says maybe. Time drips away. The homeowner wants to know whether the pool contractor can begin by March 1; the contractor says maybe. The contractor asks the homeowner whether the latest proposed design for the decorative tile work is okay; the homeowner says maybe.

In negotiation, "maybe" will bury you with wasted time, energy, money, and, the real killer, emotion. Did he really mean yes? Are we almost there? Or is he just trying a last-minute ploy for concessions? Or did he really mean no, so this offer doesn't have a chance? Or did he actually mean maybe, because he doesn't even know what he wants? What will they do if I cut my price? What will they do if I increase my order? Probably say maybe! Who the heck has any idea? It's nothing but a guessing game, and the brain is stuck and spinning its wheels with no traction because it has nothing to justify or reject.

I cannot emphasize this point too strongly: "Maybe" is the kiss of death for a successful negotiation—perhaps even for your business. Believe me, I've coached businesspeople who, when they started analyzing their own activities, realized that the essential problem was that they allowed other people to string them along with an endless series of "maybe, maybe, maybe." One woman in particular, Margaret, a wonderful person, sweet, hardworking, had initial success in her office interior design business but soon found herself curiously unable to move her customers to a decision, one way or the other. She was afraid to hear no, so "maybe" sounded great. But based on many "maybes," she purchased and was stuck with a large and expensive inventory. Bankruptcy followed. Perhaps this sounds a bit pat and far-fetched to you. I wish it were. Bottom line: Margaret's company failed, as do many others, because she was unable to get beyond all the "maybes," both hers and those of her customers.

If you can't quickly get past "maybe"—and it comes in infinite varieties, of course—start walking, because you're wasting your time.

Test Drive Find the opportunity in some harmless setting to say maybe (if not in so many words) in response to every question, every suggestion, and every issue. See how frustrating and silly this is for everyone? At another opportunity, interpret every answer to your every question as a "maybe." Do you get anywhere? I'm betting you don't.

"YES" IS NOT ANY BETTER

"Bill, this software is just what we need. I'm sure we'll buy it. Just give me a few days to run it by my partners. But I'm sure it'll fly. It's a great tool. Give me a call at the end of the week."

Bill, the salesman, calls this potential buyer at the end of the week, and you know what he probably hears. "Hey Bill, I'm going to try to get this in the budget for us. Could you give me a call next month on this?"

Consider this scenario of a different sort:

"John, will you straighten up your room? Your grandparents are coming for dinner."

"Sure, Mom. Don't worry."

Does John straighten up his room? He does not. So why did he say yes? The easy way out. Buying some time. He wants to be left alone, has no intention of straightening up his room, doesn't want to get into an argument with his mother, and knows that saying no won't work and saying maybe won't work (it can work in many negotiations, but not when he's up against Mom), so he just says yes with no intention of carrying through. The "yes" doesn't really mean anything. It's not written in blood. It's just another word to deploy at the right time.

Bill, the salesman, is dealing with the same kind of obstructionism with the "yes" he received. His customer isn't in a position to buy the software, but in the standard American way doesn't want to just say so. He doesn't want to say no. He could say maybe, and many customers would say maybe, but even better is "yes." This way he can delay saying no until he can blame the answer on someone else and not seem to be the bad guy.

Here is a related story from my own experience, when I was fundraising for high school football teams in California. I had been recommended to a new school by a coach at another school with whom I had worked successfully. That coach went so far as to make a call on my behalf to the coach at the new school. When I then called the coach of this prospective school to introduce myself, he immediately said, "Say no more, Jim. We want to work with you. When can you begin our program?"

"Next week," I said.

He paused and then replied, "Call me on Monday and we'll set it up."

I had a great weekend. I was excited to know I would start the week with a new program on Monday. It would be a great week. However, I knew in my heart that this was a weak position to be in. I knew I had not done a good job with this, but I had high hopes. After all, I am a very positive person and my expectations were through the roof. Sure this will work out! When I called the coach bright and early Monday morning, he was dutifully apologetic as he told me that the season was in full swing, and it would be better if we talked another time. "How about three weeks from now?" he asked. My heart dropped, but what could I say? (I will tell you later exactly what I should have said.) It was my fault. I would have been better off with the straight "no," but I could and should have taken the initial "yes" for what it was worth—nothing—and made the call on Monday with no neediness or high hopes whatsoever. But I made the classic mistake of thinking that "yes" meant "yes." In the end, I never did any fundraising for this coach's school.

The "maybe" response all too often gives you a thought that something good is going to happen, but it actually hampers your decision process, as it throws you into a tailspin of emotions. The same holds for "yes," which serves only to get your emotions going—to the detriment of your decision-making. When the other side says yes, you get excited, your adrenaline starts pumping, you start computing the commission and deciding between the Mercedes and the Beemer, and before you know it, you're . . . what? Needy. You *need* this deal, this low-hanging fruit. This happens very often to many. Think about it from the other perspective: How many times have you caught *yourself* saying yes to the very first question you're asked? You're trying to be agreeable and trying to keep the conversation going, and "yes" is just a harmless habit. I don't know all the reasons we're quick to say yes, but many of us are, which tells you all you need to know about what it's worth.

Do not let the quick "yes" fool you. If it does happen to be real and final—it's not likely, but it is possible—you'll find out soon enough, proceeding cautiously, without high hopes or neediness. Usually it's *not* real and final. It's either just something friendly for the other person to say, or there's something more insidious going on. The quick "yes" may be designed by the other party to set you up, to build your neediness, to undermine your decision-making. Then it's followed by the subtle "if," "but," "however," "when," or some other dangerous qualifier. Now what do you do? You're needy and you've lost your focus and become vulnerable to bad decisions—and maybe to making an unnecessary compromise. The other side is suddenly in control. Offering an early "yes" is a reliable "tiger trick," as I call it, used by polished negotiators taking advantage of weak win-win negotiators. It traps you in their cage. Shrewd negotiators use the "yes" trick all the time.

"Sure, Frank, we're on board. We want to place the biggest order ever with Acme—50,000 widgets." Frank is over the moon. This is a career-maker. Then, one or two calls later, "I didn't even bring it up, Frank. It seemed unnecessary. I'm assuming about a twenty percent discount at that volume. Is that what you have in mind?"

Never fall for the quick "yes." Assume nothing. Avoid the emotional roller coaster. Don't get needy. Don't "chase the results" that *seem* to be shimmering so invitingly right in front of your eyes. Proceed carefully under the principles of your system.

Test Drive Find the opportunity to say yes in response to every question, every suggestion, and every issue. Do your friendly "yeses" do the conversation any good, really? Is there any real progress or meeting of the minds? I'm betting otherwise. I'm betting the conversation soon becomes ridiculous. Now interpret every *answer* to your every question as a "yes." Do you see how all of these "yeses" from the other side wouldn't get you anywhere at all?

GETTING TO "NO"

If "maybe" and the quick "yes" are worthless or even dangerous, what are you left with? The most powerful word in your negotiating vocabulary: "no." "No" is a decision. That's it. It starts the process of building vision (the subject of Chapter 5). You or the other side may change the decision later. Right now, it doesn't matter. With "no," you've made real progress, because "no" induces you and the party across the table into actually thinking about why you or they have just said no. Your brains now have to justify what has been said and either accept or

reject it. The naysayer has to take responsibility for "no." Eluci-
dation is required. Now you have real issues to discuss. The
negotiation can move forward, unlike with "maybe" or the
quick "yes." But with "no," you know where you stand, you
can ask good questions (the subject of Chapter 6), and you can
move ahead.

We've been taught to fear the word, while politely saying
no, calmly hearing no, and simply inviting no from the other
side has a remarkably beneficial impact on any negotiation. As
I also said in the Introduction and repeat again here, the "no"
principle is *not* about intransigence. Just the opposite. It's
about openness and honesty. The invitation to "no" tells everyone at the table that we're all adults here, so let's talk rationally.
Let's slow things down. Let's take away the fear of failure. "No"
allows everyone involved to put away the need to be right, to
be the strongest, to be the smartest, to be the toughest. It allows us to put aside the need to feel safe and secure and liked
by the other side, and it prevents us from making terrible decisions because we need to feel safe and secure and liked. "No"
says to everyone at the table, "Let's bury any rush to judgment
born of the getting-to-yes-mentality." "No" says, "Relax, I'm not
trying to fleece you, and you're not about to fleece me."

A polite "no" does *not* offend people. On the contrary. It invites adult behavior. It opens the way for good decisions. After
all my years coaching clients in every imaginable kind of negotiation, I can still be surprised by the almost magical power
of "no."

You may remember Ross Perot, world-class businessman
and iconoclastic third-party presidential candidate in 1992 and
1996. He became famous for his big ears and his straight talk.
Convinced (or just hopeful) that American voters weren't
quite as stupid as their politicians seemed to think they were,
he gave lectures about economic issues complete with charts
and graphs. He lost to Bill Clinton, but he made an impact.
Perot enjoyed (and may still, I don't know) telling business au-

diences the story of an American who wants to buy a camel and pulls up at a tent with half a dozen of the beasts staked out front. When the owner emerges, the American asks the owner about one particular animal. The Bedouin replies, "Oh, that's my son's camel, his pet. I couldn't sell that one." The American looks nonplussed, climbs back into his Range Rover, and starts to drive off. The Bedouin runs after him, shouting, "I thought you wanted to buy my camel!"

I agree with Ross Perot: Americans don't know how to negotiate. They don't want to hear no, they don't want to say no, and they have a false definition of "no." But "no" is extremely valuable. "No" can help you control any neediness you may be tempted to feel. It establishes respect for everyone. It leads to the gathering of information. The "no" principle is *not* about getting tough. It simply gets everyone out of the guessing mode.

> **"No" gets you past emotional issues and trivial issues to decisions on essential issues. We want decision-based negotiation, not an emotion-based waste of time.**

Test Drive Have some fun and take the opportunity to practice using "no" to lighten up the moment. With a smile on your face, tell someone in a low-risk situation that you just can't do that, or that you just don't see it that way, but encourage him or her to go on. Say no, and in the next breath, encourage the person to convince you that what he or she is proposing is the right course. Or go the other way and tell the person that you have an idea and you want him or her to be comfortable saying no to you. Promise the person that he or she won't hurt your feelings. Please just tell me no. In either case, you will see the results instantly.

CASES IN POINT

John, a first-year law student, was applying for a summer internship with a very prestigious law firm in New York City. Like all valuable law school students, he had been approached with solicitation letters from excellent firms around the country. When the recruiters from the firms came to campus, he identified four he would like to have the opportunity to work with for the summer and possibly join after graduation. John was an excellent student but not at the top of his class and was concerned that his ranking might affect the outcome of his discussions. John began discussions like this: "Sir, thank you for the opportunity to speak with you. Before we begin, I would like you to know two things. First, I am not the top student in my class, and second, when we finish, if I am not who you are looking for, I would like you to just tell me no, that I am not a fit. I hope you will see that as fair."

John said the same thing to each of the four interviewers. All four accepted John's comments in a very positive way. Two said they appreciated his candor and they liked the idea that he was interested in saving time with knowing their decision. John was given second interviews by all four firms, at which point he repeated the process. Of the four he visited in New York, John received three internship offers. During the summer, while serving as an intern, John was offered a position upon graduation. He accepted and was asked to start full-time one month after graduation with the top firm he wanted.

I was contacted via e-mail by a prospective new client in Poland whose company was in the earliest stages of negotiating a vital contract with an American firm. I will call my counterpart Lech (in honor of Lech Walesa, the hardheaded shipyard worker whose Solidarity movement brought down the Communist government in Poland and helped mightily in the dissolution of the Soviet bloc). Our first five e-mails were of a getting-to-know-you nature, and I concluded that exploratory phase with an official proposal, including my fee structure. In his next e-mail, Lech replied (edited for clarity and length):

> *Dear Jim,*
>
> *Thank you for your proposal. Concerning coaching for our staff, the price of $xxx + costs is for us out of reach. We would love to be your students, but please look at the difference in GDP per head in the U.S. and Poland. Your number is not in our league. . . . Our main problem right now is getting our negotiation going. We plan to go to the U.S. Oct 15 to present our proposal. Therefore I would like to talk to you over the phone. If you can convince us you can help us with that proposal, we can work together on the process. If they accept our proposal in principle and start negotiations, this will take maybe a year, and we will probably need your help.*
>
> *Please share with us your thoughts.*
>
> Regards

In short, Lech was saying no to the numbers in my proposal and at the same time inviting me to dig into my compromise bag to see if I could come up with some money for him. So the ball was in my court, and I did review the fee I had proposed. I decided again that they were very reasonable numbers, even considering GDP issues. I did want to visit Poland, so I had a little emotional baggage here, but I decided to reject Lech's invitation to compromise, for the simple reason that the fee I had proposed was fair.

I wrote him a brief note: "Lech, I wish you all the best. Good luck with the negotiation. Best wishes, Jim." That was my "no" in reply to his "no." Was that the end of this little negotiation? Did he walk away? Was he mad at me? Was he offended? In no way. Within three hours Lech replied, "Jim, any comments to my letter? Regards, Lech."

He was acknowledging that I had said no and declined to compromise, and he was inviting me to think about everything again. My "no" hadn't ended the negotiation. I decided to explain to Lech the real problem, as I saw it. Given the difficulty of the negotiation he was heading into and given the language and cultural problems, he required labor-intensive, hands-on training. I knew from experience that in order for this training to be effective, his commitment would be necessary, and he would not have that commitment unless he paid my fee. People who hire a coach and pay for coaching work harder. That's a fact. Money equals commitment. In order to execute my coaching in his company's upcoming difficult and protracted negotiation, Lech would have to make some tough decisions. If he wouldn't pay my fee—a tough decision, apparently— would he be able to make *other* tough decisions? Very doubtful, so my answer to him was simple: "Lech, without training I can't help you. I wish you the best." And I did. Nice guy.

Lech had now received two "noes" from me—and continued to negotiate. His next note tried even more persuasion, at some length. It began, "Jim, I think it must be my English. I did not say I do not want your coaching. I do." He then laid out the pressing time issues and the two phases of his negotiation with the American firm, which would involve some complex swapping of shares. Then he asked me, in effect, how he should proceed in the first stage of the negotiation with the American firm, and how that approach might dovetail with my fee. Apparently, he wanted me to divide my fee into two stages, corresponding to the stages of the upcoming negotiation.

My gut told me to say no, but beware the gut—the emotions—so I stepped back to think about that "gut decision." And I came to the same conclusion. I would only be comfortable with my fee structure as proposed, and I doubted whether Lech would make the commitment to coaching without making the first decision to pay that fee. So my next "no" was an easy call for me. My note said, "Lech, I wish you the best. Without payment I cannot engage. All the best . . ."

That was my final "no." If we were going to work together, Lech would have to come around to the relationship between coaching and commitment. And Lech just didn't get it. His next note read, "Jim, last try. I want to pay you for the first part separately, then for the second part. The first part will require some time involvement, the second substantially more. Regards . . ."

Another "no" from him, and that was that. The negotiation was over. We did not have a deal. We were never going to have a deal. Lech wanted a two-tier payment structure, and I don't work that way. The key point for the discussion here is that the way Lech and I got to that understanding was *through the use of "no."* If you go back and look at those exchanges, you'll see that if the two of us had exchanged a series of "maybes," we'd still be going around and around to this very day, probably without knowing much more about where we stood than we did in the beginning. And a bunch of "yeses" from each of us would have led to a waste of time before we got around to the "buts." (Lech's: "Yes, but I want to pay you in two stages." Jim's: "Yes, but I need to see your commitment, and paying my fee structure is the first part of that commitment.")

It was so much simpler with the "noes." They moved things right along. They required us to think about what we were saying. No one walked away in anger.

Here's how confident I am about the power of "no":

Test Drive One day when you're trying to get Johnny to agree to some onerous chore that will surely ruin his weekend, if not his life, right when you've reached the "closing" stage of this negotiation, try something different. Instead of nailing down the agreement in what is probably your normal way, with some kind of hard declaration — "Okay, Johnny, I expect you to mow the lawn this afternoon. You just promised" — try the opposite. Don't "close" him at all. Instead, give him the right to say "no": "Are you sure, Johnny? You're okay with this? Now's the time to speak up." You may be pleasantly surprised with the results. I know I was.

About a dozen years ago, my son Jim had some time after he

graduated from college and before he began his training to become an Air Force pilot. To begin a career in the civilian world
that he could return to after his military experience, Jim went
to work with about fifty other men and women cold-calling for
Prudential Brokerage in New York. On the first day, Jim said
he wasn't going to use the self-defeating script he was given,
which went something like this: "Hello, Mr. Smith. I am Jim
Camp and I represent Prudential Brokerage. We offer the finest
in securities to substantial investors like yourself. I would like
to sit down with you and show you all we could do for you
with our vast array of products. Would three on Tuesday or four
on Wednesday be best?"

Instead, Jim said he wanted to use a script of his own (and
my) devising, one that included an invitation to say no. It read,
"Hello, Mr. Smith. My name is Jim Camp. I am not sure if what
we do fits in your world. If it doesn't, just let me know and I
will get off the phone. Is that fair? . . . Mr. Smith, whom do you
have in your corner helping you with your investments? I am
with Prudential Brokerage, and I'd like the opportunity to sit
down with you and allow you to discover the opportunities."

Okay, his manager said about Jim's different script, but
you'd better produce. Jim did produce—about three times
what anyone else in that office accomplished. In fact, just one
new client moved him to the head of his class:

> One of my first actual appointments on that job was
> with a potential client named Bob. As I was preparing
> to meet him for the first time, my branch manager
> pulled me into his office for his usual pep talk. "Just
> sell him some bonds," he said. "That's a great way to
> get a new account." I had a different approach in
> mind. I wasn't going to meet him just for the sake of
> offering something for him to buy. If I was going to
> work with him, it would be because I could provide a
> great service and he could feel comfortable in always

being able to say no. I knew from my appointment call that Bob was retired. I also knew he was a very conservative investor. His home was much older and more modest than I expected. After the usual pleasantries, Bob invited me to sit down at the kitchen table. "What are you going to sell me today?" he immediately asked. I'll never forget the relief on his face when I said, "Well, Bob, I can't make any recommendations until I have a clear picture of your situation. Let's see if there's a fit here. If either of us determines that there's not, we'll simply go our separate ways. Fair enough? How comfortable are you discussing your investments with me?"

I truly did not know if I could help Bob. After a long discussion, we concluded that his investments were doing well and that a change wasn't really necessary. We ended the appointment with an agreement to stay in touch, in case his situation changed. Returning to the office, I could already hear my boss declaring, "Just get the account!" He said that and more. He warned that I'd never make it in the business if I didn't sell more aggressively. Less than an hour later, while I was making more cold calls, someone called me. Bob. I immediately thought I must have left something at his home. Instead, he asked if I was familiar with the ACAT form necessary to transfer brokerage accounts. As matter of fact, yes. And my heart jumped just a tiny bit, I admit. Then Bob said he was going to transfer his account to Prudential—his entire portfolio, which was scattered across six different brokerage houses. He said I was the only broker he'd ever come across whom he trusted. I hadn't tried to force anything. I hadn't tried to "close" him. He did not want to do much trading, he added, so I wouldn't make much in commissions from the account, but he was going to recommend to his entire family to work with me when he was gone.

The new hires at the firm were supposed to bring in $10 million in assets under management, quite a large number considering that the typical new account at the time was less than $10,000. Following that phone call, Bob delivered $6 million in assets. What would have happened if I'd walked into his kitchen *needing* to open an account or if I'd chased results and followed my boss's instructions to close the deal? What if I had not given Bob every opportunity to say no? He would never have called back.

That was quite a coup for my son but no surprise at all for me. The power of "no" never surprises me.

RELATIONSHIPS

It is shocking how many people misuse the word "relationship" and therefore put themselves at risk. I've lost count of how many times I've been asked, "How will people *like* my company if we don't offer a discount?" In just so many words! Not "How will my company be profitable by becoming a more effective, dynamic company with which to do business?" Instead, "How will they like us?" or "I have to maintain this relationship." It's amazing how many negotiators want to be liked, want to "save the relationship" with the other side, or want to save the other side from making a tough decision. Just imagine the tough negotiators lying in wait to take advantage of such a weak, vulnerable mindset and approach. It happens every day—and in the story I tell next, this one day almost ruined the preceding six months of the negotiation.

This had been a difficult negotiation. Lou and his team were working on the agreement with a potential distributor of their products in the Asian market. As each item was agreed upon during the last round of negotiations and the teams closed in on the final issue—price, not surprisingly—everyone could feel the emotions creeping into the picture. A dangerous moment was at hand. The potential distributor wanted another 7 percent of the distributed price, while Lou and his team where holding the line. Lou had said no in just about every way imaginable on this question. During a Mother Nature break, Hiro, a high-level member of the other team, approached Ken, one of the lower-level members of Lou's team, and intimated that this impasse would derail the negotiation. Ken fell for this gambit. He told Hiro that he would recommend to Lou that they meet in the middle, if Hiro thought it would help. Hiro said, "Ken san, this effort at good partnership should solve the problem, save the relationship, and save the negotiation. It is good to see someone willing to keep the negotiation alive and save the relationship."

Ken then asked Lou and the team if they could meet separately before the negotiation resumed. He told Lou what had happened: If they split the difference on the 7 percent, they had a deal. You know Lou's reaction—that 3.5 percent difference represented $30 million—but Lou also immediately understood that he had made his own mistake: leaving a younger member of the team alone with a high-level member of the other team. That would never happen again, with Ken or anyone else, but the more immediate problem was this unauthorized compromise. What to do, because Lou was determined to not make it. His position was a solid one. The mission and purpose and the business proposal on the table were solid. The numbers were right.

Unlike his man Ken, Lou did not waver. When the meeting resumed, he stated the new problem very clearly. Ken had made a completely unauthorized "decision." Lou could not split the difference. Of course he'd be disappointed if the six months already spent on the negotiation went down the drain (my phrase, not his), but he understood that Ken's mistake was a bad one, and if Hiro and his team felt they now had to reject the last official proposal, Lou would understand. He even offered to adjourn the session until the following day, if Hiro needed the time. Hiro asked for two weeks. Everyone went home. Then Hiro called Lou and said that the business with Ken was unfortunate, but he wanted to complete the agreement based on the final terms as Lou had presented them.

Never take responsibility for the other side's decisions. Never "save the relationship."

Without question, one of the most dangerous mistakes you can make in any negotiation is trying to "save" the other party from the tough decisions—as I put it, "saving the friendly relationship." There can be no saving of the other party, not emotionally, intellectually, financially, or on any other level. No. None. Never. There can be *no* saving the relationship. It's a terrible practice that does neither side any good. *Neither side?* That's correct, because if you do save the other side, *you* are now partially responsible for *their* decision. If some problem comes up later, who gets the guilt trip laid on them? You may hear, "Well, *you* are the one who convinced me to do this. You gave me a deal I couldn't refuse, knowing it wouldn't work. It's your fault. This will never happen again."

Taking responsibility for others' decisions will always set you up for trouble, but some form of saving the relationship— almost always with an unnecessary compromise—happens *hourly,* all over the world, in all fields of endeavor. I have a client Dan, who runs the implementation team for a software company that provides solutions to government clients nationally and internationally. In the episode I have in mind, Dan was negotiating with Doris, a consultant hired by a very large European city to ensure a smooth transition and implementation of the new software. But Doris didn't want to sign the contract for implementation. She bluntly told Dan that her word was good enough and that she never stooped so low as to sign a contract. Her exact words were "contracts are for people who can't be trusted." To solidify her position, she enlisted the aid of Harold, Dan's colleague with whom she had previously worked. Harold came to Doris's defense on the contract issue and jumped all over Dan for taking a position that insulted such a major player in the consulting world.

Harold didn't want to hurt his long-standing rapport with Doris. He didn't want to hurt her feelings by joining his own colleague in saying, quite reasonably, "This is our policy. Without a signed contract, we cannot take the financial responsibility for your implementation." His desire to save the relationship with Doris had turned him into an in-house saboteur, in effect, putting Dan and his implementation team in the position of taking a considerable financial risk. That contract was signed in the end and five others followed. The relationship, based solely on business, is now stronger than ever.

Here's an important question, and another point of that story: Wasn't this a case in which the negotiator on the other side did *not* react positively when she heard the word "no"? Yes, it was. Doesn't this story therefore contradict my entire claim that "no" frees up a negotiation and induces everyone to act like adults and make responsible decisions? Only in a very limited way. Doris did not appreciate hearing no. This is true. She could not accept it when Dan required a fully executed contract. In a long phone monologue, she said she'd never been treated like this. She accused Dan of discounting her experience and reputation and integrity. She saw Dan's "no" as representing a lack of trust. She simply couldn't accept it. She did *seem* to take the politest imaginable "no" as personal rejection. Or was she playing some kind of game of emotional guilt? Almost every time, in my experience, people reacting as Doris did are indeed playing the guilt game. Specifically, they're playing you for a sucker, figuring your guilt and blame will take over when you run into their negativism. They figure you'll panic and then try to—what else?—*save the relationship*. Trained negotiators use this ploy all the time against timid negotiators. It's easy to do, because the unspoken—or sometimes spoken—

assumption behind a compromise-based mindset is that people enter negotiations trying to build friendly relationships and want to leave with that friendly relationship intact.

The classic compromise mindset dilemma is this one: *What can I give in order to gain or maintain this friendly relationship?* Big-time corporate negotiators play up the importance of relationships for the long term using concepts like partnership, loyalty, trust, and dislike of arrogant suppliers—emotion-based stuff. *How could you endanger such benefits by taking this position?* But their only real concern is the price they're paying. And pretty soon you change your position.

A client once said to me, "Oh, I'm good friends with their head of purchasing."

"Really? That's interesting."

"Yeah, his wife and my wife are pretty good friends, too. They play tennis."

"Really! How long have you had this relationship?"

"Five or six years, I guess."

"How long has he been head of purchasing?"

Pause. "Five or six years, I guess."

True story. You and I both know it happens. An explicit strategy of some corporate negotiating teams is to use outings and junkets and all other means to establish friendships that can then be used as unspoken leverage when the going gets tough. Friendships with the good folks on the other side can be fine—or they can be dangerous. It's hard enough for many negotiators to say no to people they've just met. How much harder is it to say no to friends?

RESPECT, NOT FRIENDSHIP

The impulse to think and act in any such save-the-relationship fashion is wrongheaded not only because it's bad negotiating but also because the people across the table do *not* want to be your friend. They could not care less. *They have not even thought about it.* Now, I noted earlier in this chapter that most of us want to be liked, don't want to hurt feelings, and don't want to be blunt or surly or arrogant. Nor do we want to be on the *receiving* end of such behavior. But this does not mean that we want to be everybody's best friend. For businesspeople and negotiators in any field, much more important than friendliness are effectiveness and respect. Nothing more.

Have you ever wondered how the jerks of the world get along? How some even get ahead? How more than a few even get to the very top? These people don't get away with their boorish, offensive behavior for any good reason. They get away with it because they're effective in their work and bring benefit to their business relationships, in one way or another. Every reader of this book understands exactly what I'm saying here. You can think of a case in which you've chosen to deal with a somewhat obnoxious but effective person rather than a friendly but ineffective one. What does friendship have to do with making good business and negotiation decisions? Not a thing. In your negotiations, you must be polite and respectful with everyone at all times. This is mandatory. But this practice has nothing to do with *saving* them from taking responsibility for their decisions, all for the sake of some unwanted friendship or for being liked or for feeling important. Most businesspeople, if they stop to think about this question carefully, will agree that friendships in business are the product of long-term effective dealings. Making decisions based on a sense that someone seeks your friendship is misguided. He or she would much prefer your effectiveness.

Why would you want to load down a business relationship with a lot of emotional baggage, including guilt, which can be the by-product of "friendship"? It doesn't work. It doesn't pay. If your agreements result from effective decision-making, the odds are very good that there will be a long-term business relationship, regardless of whether you play golf with the people. If your agreements are the result of ineffective decision-making, there won't be—and should not be—a long-term relationship, no matter how many rounds you play.

Test Drive Find a simple opportunity to say to the other party, "James, I can't be your *friend* here. I'd prefer that you *respect* me, and I think that's probably what you would prefer, too. And I respect you. That's why I'm not going to beat around the bush. My company just can't do that." James can handle this "no." You'll see.

THE *NEXT* DECISION

Another reason people are afraid to say no is that they fear making the wrong decision. This fear of the wrong decision is one of the most debilitating emotions of all, burrowing deep beneath all aspects of decision-making, because it strikes a chord with our fear of failing. Inexperienced or compromise-based negotiators believe that "no" locks them into a wrong decision from which they wouldn't be able to recover. In school, all the kids are afraid of giving a wrong answer in class because they'll be embarrassed and then laughed at by the other kids. In the business world, adults are beset by fear that the wrong answer—the wrong decision—can ruin the negotiation, their entire career. *Unnecessary* fear of a bad decision is a major stumbling block to good decisions.

> "I just don't know. Should I or shouldn't I?"

> "What if I can do better?"

> "I don't know. The whole thing sounds too good."

> "This seems so easy. Maybe I can win even more."

> "What are they up to? Why are they making this so easy?"

"What do they know that I don't know?"

"This just can't be right."

"This is going all wrong. How can I get out of this?"

Each of these qualms and hundreds more are evidence that the negotiator is beset by doubts about a decision because of the fear of being wrong. How do you get rid of this fear? I'll answer this question with another one: What really happens when you make a bad decision? There is a common saying among pilots: "Flying is a continuous string of decisions, most of them bad ones that must be corrected." In training, pilots are told to just keep making decisions and pretty soon they will get it right.

To be effective decision-makers we must simply make *the next decision,* and then the next one, and then the next one. A negotiation is a series of decisions. When—not if, but when— you make a bad decision, you simply follow it with a better one. Understanding this simple lesson will liberate you as a negotiator. Take responsibility for the bad decision, learn from it, embrace the failure, and soldier on without fear, because you are only one decision away from getting back on track. But this attitude and approach take discipline and a lot of self-confidence, because "being right" is very important to most of us. It is a powerful *need,* and like all needs, it must be overcome.

Mike found himself in just such a situation. He's a senior VP at Zete, a manufacturing firm specializing in data communications. For three months, a procurement team from Turbo, a Fortune 100 company, had been demanding reimbursement from Zete for a defective product replaced at considerable cost. The team to which Mike had delegated the response examined the expense spreadsheet provided by the other company, calculated that Zete owed $3.7 million, and informed Turbo that a proposal would be forthcoming to resolve the matter.

Mike was surprised and disappointed. Wasn't this a warranty matter, and wasn't the allegedly defective product out of warranty? So how did Zete owe Turbo anything? Zete had fulfilled the entire contract and had the records to prove it. John, the team leader, explained to Mike that the procurement folks had made it clear that they wanted Mike to cover the loss, even if it was a bogus deal. Otherwise, Zete would be locked out at Turbo in the future. John also admitted to Mike that he had already told the Turbo group that he would recommend payment. If Zete didn't pay now, John would be in a very awkward position—a figure without authority, unable to deliver on a promise and almost a liar. Zete wouldn't look very good either.

Thanks to John's bad decision as a result of pressure from procurement, the refusal to pay a false claim could have several nasty repercussions. This was a tough spot for Mike. He immediately asked Larry, one of his vice presidents, to take over for John, reopen the negotiation, and fix all the problems. Larry jumped at the opportunity and asked for a meeting with Karen, who was handling Turbo's request for reimbursement. Karen wouldn't take the meeting. She asked Larry to deliver the proposal to pay as promised by John. Here is the actual e-mail she wrote:

> Larry, I have spoken with my management on this issue and at this time we do not feel that another senior-level meeting is necessary/warranted. Zete has met with both CV and GM a number of times with no proposal back from Zete to support this issue. Our expectation is that you will provide a proposal to support the BI012 out-of-pocket expenses that have been provided to your team a number of times. We are looking for Zete to correct the out-of-pocket expenses that have been created because of failures in your components/manufacturing process. Please provide me with an expected response date. Karen.

Okay, a firm "no." Fair enough. Larry waited two days, then repeated his request for a meeting with Karen, stating, "A new team is in place and in charge and it is impossible to issue a proposal without knowing what has happened and what should happen in the future." Karen's turn to hear "no." Another "no," another exchange of information, and another decision. This time the meeting is granted. Karen realizes there is a new team in this negotiation and a proposal will not be forthcoming. It will take a new meeting and engagement to get what she wants.

As the meeting unfolded, Larry assured Karen and Turbo that Zete was very interested in maintaining a strong relationship with Turbo, but he did *not* offer to pay the $3.7 million in order to do so. Instead, he did a great job of asking the right questions and gathering information (both subjects of upcoming chapters), and he promised to get back in touch soon to resolve the matter. As it turned out, Larry now had all the ammunition he needed to confirm Mike's conviction that Zete didn't owe Turbo a dime. The request for reimbursement was completely out of line. Convinced that something was rotten at Turbo, Larry asked Mike to elevate this negotiation to the very highest levels of both companies. Mike did that, and Turbo's leadership ended up agreeing with Larry's analysis. They removed Karen from the scene. Soon enough, the companies signed new deals to the tune of $180 million—all thanks to the fact that Mike wasn't afraid to make a "next" decision after the original terrible decision. Not incidentally, that next decision was "no."

One of my favorite illustrations of the "next decision" lesson is Coca-Cola's decision years ago to change their formula, when they came on the market with the "New Coke." We can all imagine the time and care and marketing research that must have gone into such an important decision regarding the most famous brand on the planet. Nevertheless, they got it wrong— terribly wrong. What a killer decision, an unbelievably embarrassing decision. But not the end of the world. When Coke drinkers unanimously shouted *"No!"* the company simply reversed the decision. (Or was that first decision actually an unbelievably clever marketing ploy? I've heard that theory, which holds that the company replaced Classic Coke with New Coke in order to remind us how much we love the real thing. Either way—blunder or ploy—the move worked out well, because sales soared, along with the company's capitalization.)

A second favorite illustration from the annals of big-time business is Microsoft, which was dead wrong for years in its dismissive attitude toward the Internet. When Bill Gates realized his error, he turned his giant company of 15,000 employees on a dime. Within 90 days, every division of Microsoft reenvisioned its mission and purpose in terms of the Net. Whatever your feelings about the Man from Microsoft, you have to acknowledge that this was an incredible demonstration of business leadership. He wasn't going to persevere in a bad decision (or a nondecision, actually). He did an about-face and nobody thinks the less of him for it (though some observers and competitors think the less of him for other reasons, jealousy among them).

ONE LAST TIME

Embrace "no" at every opportunity in a negotiation. Don't fear the word—invite it. You do *not* take it as a personal rejection, because you are not needy. You understand that every "no" is *reversible*. The moment you really internalize this principle, the moment you understand the honesty and the *power* of "no," you will have taken a long stride away from emotion-based negotiating toward decision-based negotiating. The moment you quit worrying about whether you will hurt someone's feelings, the moment you quit trying to save a relationship, you will be a much better negotiator.

You say maybe or even a false "yes," and believe that these answers solve everyone's problem, because they keep the game going and because you haven't had to say the nasty word and they haven't had to hear it. Win-win? No. Lose-lose, because with "maybe" and a quick "yes," an easy "yes," what do you accomplish, really? Nothing. They do not move you forward. They waste time. You remain mired in the win-win mindset, certain to be victimized by it sooner than later.

If you cannot accept "no," you will burn too many bridges and have no way back with too many negotiations. *Nothing*—absolutely nothing—is more important to a successful negotiation than for you to make as clear as possible from the very beginning that "no" is a perfectly acceptable response at this negotiating table. You must make clear that you do not take "no" as a personal rejection, but as an honest decision that can be discussed and perhaps reversed.

This can be difficult to do when dealing with experienced negotiators, but when you are able to do it, you'll be amazed how this right to say and hear no clears the air at the negotiating table. If the negotiators are shrewd, highly trained experts, they may huff and puff and go negative. They might even call you a bad partner, incompetent, or unethical, because you didn't cave in and agree, but they'll also consider you with a great deal more respect. If they're naïve or weak negotiators, they will feel much safer. They can give you an honest "no," you'll accept it gratefully, and they know you'll react in the same way in the future. Feeling safe saying no, they also feel safe hearing no. Barriers go down and trust goes up. Everyone feels more comfortable and everyone becomes more forthright. We're all adults here, so the atmosphere of honesty is welcome.

In the long run, "no" is really the safest answer. It does *not* tear down business relationships. It *builds* them. You want a strong agreement, a lasting agreement, an agreement that moves you forward. Saying and inviting and hearing "no" is the foundation of great agreements.

Three-Minute Checklist

- If you're needy, it's hard to say no and it's hard to hear no. Check for neediness first.
- If you have saddled yourself with performance goals over which you have no control, it's hard to say no and it's hard to hear no.
- Before anything happens, before the meeting starts, are you firmly free in your gut and in your mind to say no and hear no? If not, cancel the meeting. Seriously.

4

The Greatest Negotiation
Secret Ever

Rooting Your Mission and Purpose
in the World of the Other Side

'm amazed every time I ask people to identify their mission
and purpose (M&P). Over and over I hear, *Well, I want to
make a million dollars. . . . I want to make the team. . . . I want to
sign the deal. . . . I want to get this job.* Such statements are pretty
standard, and you will recognize them as performance goals
over which the individual does not exert control. They can
only lead to the futile habit of chasing results, as discussed in
Chapter 2. Such statements about *money* and *gratification* and
power don't get you very far in negotiation, not over the long
haul, because the other side isn't interested in your ambitions.
People make a big mistake confusing mission and purpose
with money and power. The other side wants to know what
you bring to the table to benefit *them,* and your M&P must be
focused likewise. At the corporate level, the innocuous, generic
M&P statement cooked up by the marketing people for use in
the annual report is probably a waste of time and words; if it
doesn't guide actual, nitty-gritty decision-making, it can even

be counterproductive. Now you must forget all such exercises in self-deception. I teach and coach a working mission and purpose, a mission and purpose that will drive decisions. Here's the key difference:

> **In any negotiation, your mission and purpose**
> **must be rooted *in the world of the other side*.**

If you're a salesperson, your mission and purpose is not about selling 10,000 widgets and making $5 million. That's in your world. It doesn't benefit your customers at all. It's also just chasing results. In the broadest terms, a valid M&P will effectively guide your decisions. It might well be about providing your customers with a dependable widget (if not the best widget in the world) that can sustain their company's profitability well into the future, assuring their staying power and market share. See the difference? The perspective in this statement is *their* world. You're not chasing the results of your world, results you can't even control, but you do have total control over the quality of your widget. You do have control over its pricing. You do have control over your mission and purpose. It belongs to you. It is yours to change as you see fit.

We all know the phrase that is now *de rigueur* in retail sales: "The customer comes first." I'd like to know the retail company that has thrived over a long period of time with any other modus operandi. This is the reason I wonder about the long-term prospects for companies in certain industries (computers come to mind) that are taking advantage of the current boom and letting their customer service slide. They rely on those automated phone programs that serve mainly to enrage us with their endless prompts. Their websites post no phone numbers. If you can even send an e-mail, you get an automated reply, then silence. Maybe there's a list of FAQs, and maybe one of them helps; if not, you're out of luck. Or tech support is a chat line that takes an hour of back-and-forth to resolve a billing matter that would take two minutes on the phone. I think these companies may be in for a surprise when things cool off. There will be some winners and losers, and I'm betting on the companies whose mission and purpose includes careful consideration of the world in which we customers live.

Truly, a business puts consistent profits in the bank over a long period of time by putting the customer first, and there's a direct analogy with every negotiation: You make good agreements that stick only by entering heart and soul into the plans, requirements, needs, hopes, fears, and dreams of the people across the table. That's where the action is, that's where their decisions will be made—by definition—and that's where your mission and purpose must be rooted.

BUILDING THE M&P

The process of building your own mission and purpose is straightforward. It requires dedication, but it is not rocket science. The key throughout the process is to think creatively, clearly, and completely about your business and your negotiation.

1. Pull out a sheet of paper or open a new document on your computer and list the *features* of what your company, your product, or your service does—or what you do.

If you sell widgets, you will list their salient features regarding quality, durability, serviceability, industry reputation, and the like. Be creative. List anything and everything. If you're the *buyer* of the widget, you are broadening the supplier's market, increasing its sales, perhaps helping it unload inventory at certain times of the year. Keep going. There are more features, I'm sure.

If you're a parent preparing for a parent-teacher's conference regarding the recent decline in your child's math grades, the features might be your support of the teacher's decisions regarding remedial work, your willingness to engage a tutor, or your willingness to work with you child yourself every day. If you're the teacher, you are providing a structured plan for Johnny's math deficiencies, closer daily monitoring of Johnny's work in the classroom, timely reports to his parents on his progress—and more.

If you're negotiating with a specific buyer for a house with a beautiful yard, but you know for a fact that this buyer could not care less about the yard, should it be on your list of features? Not for this negotiation, but maybe for the next one.

Take your time with this process. Work on your list for a while, put it down, and come back another day. When you're reasonably confident that the list of features is complete, proceed.

2. Across from every feature on your list, write down the *benefits* of that feature for the other party.

Maybe there's a one-to-one correlation, maybe you see more than one benefit for a certain feature, maybe several features have the same benefit, or maybe the feature itself is the benefit. Don't worry about any of that. Just be sure to write down every benefit you see.

The key here is to see clearly what you provide. What benefits are you offering that solve their problems and empower them for the future? If you're the homeowner negotiating with the lawn-care service, you almost certainly bring the prospect of referrals—perhaps a significant benefit for the service. Every negotiation is different. Every negotiation has more going on than immediately meets the eye. The idea here is to end up with a *complete* description and vision of the value for the other party that you're bringing to the table.

In my experience, newcomers to this process initially overlook benefits they are bringing to the other side, and they enjoy the process of discovering them. Who wouldn't?

3. Prioritize your list of features and benefits.

What benefits do you see are most important for the other party in this negotiation? Again, immerse yourself in their world. If the teacher's main concern is that Johnny puts in supervised extra time every day on long-division problems, your willingness to supervise his efforts would probably be the number-one benefit on the list. If this teacher's number-one concern is Johnny's conduct in class, your willingness to support her disciplinary efforts might be number one on your list. If the potential home buyer has said nice things about the beautiful yard but is a zealous gourmet cook who stands over the stove all weekend, you the real estate agent don't want to neglect the yard as a benefit, but the kitchen with the Viking stove and the Sub-Zero refrigerator ends up higher on your list.

4. Now you're ready to write your M&P from the features and benefits on your final, prioritized list. Think in terms of your *continuing* task or responsibility (what you're going to do, provide, supply, or create for the benefit of the other side) and your *long-term* aim (what you're going to be, develop, or grow into long-term for the benefit of the other side).

Let's walk through an example for the widget supplier together. Our list of features and benefits might look like this:

FEATURES	BENEFITS
1. State-of-the-art widget	1. Industry-leading high speed/ low energy needs
2. Durable	2. Low maintenance/long life/savings
3. Local manufacturing	3. Low delivery cost
4. Removal shell	4. Reduced maintenance cost

If you sell widgets, your mission and purpose cannot be "to clear out my inventory," because your inventory means nothing to your customers. Instead, it might read like this:

To provide a state-of-the-art widget that delivers industry-leading higher speed to the user while providing immediate cost savings in energy and less frequent replacement and maintenance. Local manufacture will assure ease of replacement delivery and lower delivery costs.

If you're the buyer of these same widgets, the features and benefits you bring to the table might look like these:

FEATURES	BENEFITS
1. Solid customer base	1 Stable manufacturing schedule
2. Engineering support	2. R&D superiority
3. Payment on delivery	3. Solid cash flow/profit
4. Full credit/branding	4. End user market awareness

And your mission and purpose might be to provide the widget supplier with enhanced opportunity to lead the industry in market share utilizing a solid customer base awareness of their brand, to provide future growth in market share through research-and-development efforts delivered by engineering support, and to assure the supplier of the cash flow required to maintain a solid financial foundation.

❐   ❐   ❐

Interviewing for a job, your mission and purpose might be to help the employer discover it has the opportunity to enhance its team and to benefit from the strengths that you can provide. If you are a politician or some other kind of leader, your mission and purpose must be set in the world of your constituents. It might be to provide leadership that will deliver the disciplines and policies that will offer them the opportunities to achieve their objectives. Your work is not about what you want to accomplish, but about what you want your constituents to understand about you, your values, your beliefs, and your programs as you work on their behalf. And what about Jim Camp, author of this book? My mission and purpose for this book is to provide you the opportunity to discover that if you engage in training and coaching of the "No" system, you can elevate your success in negotiation to very high levels. This will be accomplished by means of clear, concise writing that is easy to read and thought-provoking. The key word here is *opportunity*. My purpose is not to elevate your success regardless. That would be a performance goal over which I do not have control. I can't be certain you'll think about the principles in my system and apply them diligently, or that you will embrace training and coaching. I can only provide you with the *opportunity* to do so. There is a huge difference, obviously, and I have no doubt at all that this book does provide that opportunity, and so I am writing it. As a coach I provide a structure that my clients can rely on, a structure that works every time when properly applied. Mission and purpose is the foundation of that structure.

> **Your mission and purpose in negotiation is your continuing task and responsibility (what you're going *to do*) and your long-term aim (what you're going *to be*), with both always grounded in the world of the other party.**

As you develop your own mission-and-purpose statement, keep in mind that all good M&P statements are concise. All must be written. What happens when you go through the process of writing anything down? I can't tell you, technically, but I do know that putting a thought into writing makes it stronger and reinforces commitment. Our minds are amazing tools, but they can lose focus. Important matters are written down for a reason, and it's not to create busywork. So pick up your pen or sit down at the keyboard. (Frankly, I think the pen is better. It slows you down. It really concentrates the mind. Try it.)

Also keep in mind that you or your company may well have

more than one M&P. You will have the overall mission and purpose for your business or enterprise, and others for guiding operations within your company. You will have a mission and purpose for your negotiation with a specific party. Within that negotiation you may have yet other layers of mission and purpose, each of which guides the decision-making at that point. In complicated, high-stakes negotiations, my clients write an M&P for almost every phone call to anyone on the other side. No kidding.

Your mission and purpose can and perhaps should *change*. At first blush, this may sound completely contradictory to every previous point here, but features and benefits change, markets change, customers change, and when they do, your mission and purpose should change accordingly. Perhaps you're a plumber and the emphasis of your business has slowly but surely switched from residential to commercial. Your mission and purpose must change. Think about how the Internet has changed the products and services that phone companies offer their customers, catalog companies offer their customers, or advertising companies offer their customers. In fact, the Internet has or should have changed the mission and purpose of most of the businesses in this economy. In the end, who will be immune to it?

As a negotiation coach, I have worked with many freelancers, sole proprietors, and owners of very small businesses who initially feel that their mission and purpose is self-evident. It's not. Without one, these individuals are working at great disadvantage. They are just as vulnerable to working and negotiating on behalf of an invalid mission and purpose as is any employee with a large multinational, and they must begin to develop one immediately.

I have also found that most people who are unhappy and frustrated in their work either have an invalid mission and purpose—"I want to make a million dollars before I'm twenty-one"—or don't have one at all and are serving *someone else's*. Working on behalf of someone else's M&P is fine *if* you understand that you are doing so, and *if* you freely embrace and take the other one as your own. It is a terrible waste, however, to work on behalf of someone else's mission and purpose without realizing it. But if you don't have one, haven't even thought about the subject, that's what is happening, and that's probably the source of your unhappiness in your job. I know quite a few lawyers, doctors, airline pilots, engineers, and some in other walks of life who give the impression, if they don't say so outright, that they'd quit tomorrow if they could think of another way to make as much money. I'm optimistic (or naïve) enough to believe that a good deal of this dissatisfaction could be allayed if they'd just dig into all the questions they need to answer in order to build a mission and purpose.

A strong, valid M&P set in the world of the other party will give you crystal-clear guidance. It gives you a disciplined, effective way of thinking and making decisions, especially the decision to say no. How can you stay on track during any kind of extended endeavor without a clear mission and purpose? It's almost impossible. There's no other way. When you do develop and adhere to a mission and purpose, how can you go fatally off the track? Again, it's almost impossible.

Test Drive Before you embark on something fairly basic—perhaps the routine Monday morning meeting of the sales reps, a standard courtesy call to a current client, or a discussion with your son about his going to summer school this year—take the time to think in broad terms about mission and purpose, about benefits brought to the table, and about your continuing task and responsibility (what you're going to do) and your long-term aim (what you're going to be), terms that will convey those benefits to the sales reps, the client, or your son. Slowly but surely, with practice, you'll see how the M&P set in the world of the other party works. You'll see tremendous value for guiding your actions and decisions. You will instinctively, intuitively consult the mission and purpose for more and more such situations, until it becomes second nature. At this stage, you *own* your mission and purpose. This is profoundly satisfying and valuable.

MISSION AND PURPOSE IN ACTION

Perhaps the most powerful product of a mission and a purpose is the insulation it provides from debilitating emotions, especially neediness. When the other party in a negotiation fires a veritable fusillade of threats, requests, deadlines, quibbles, half-truths, bogus promises, and other stuff, your mission and purpose will serve as your very own missile defense shield to deal with these tactics. *I'm feeling a lot of need here, but I have a valid mission and purpose. I know this decision does not serve that mission and purpose, so I have no qualms about calmly saying no.* If "no" is *their* decision, fine; your next move is guided by your mission and purpose.

Meet John, the inventor of a special proprietary air-conditioning unit that cools the temperature-sensitive technology in the cell phone towers that have sprouted everywhere over the last decade. Obviously, this technology is most vulnerable in the hot deserts of the Southwest, and that's where John has located his small niche company. One day he received an inquiry from the largest cell phone provider in the Middle East. There is a lot of desert in that region of the world, and a lot of money. Such a contract in that area of the world might utterly transform John's business. It might even catapult his small private company into the realm of a publicly traded international market leader. All very tempting, but he understood that he had to proceed carefully. He would not be negotiating with amateurs.

He started his work with mission and purpose. The concept of M&P was new to him—my concept, that is. He had developed the technology and his intellectual property, but he had spent little if any time thinking about his long-term responsibilities to his clients. Instead, he spent most of his time trying to guess how much he could charge for his equipment, basing his calculations on the price of off-the-rack air-conditioning units. Now he thought carefully about the features and benefits of his invention, including the vital importance for his customers of protecting their expensive, remote equipment, the value of uptime to these companies, the ease of maintenance offered, and the improved return on investment. Of course he included the importance of research and development for delivering even better air-conditioning in the future. He studied the identity of his customers and the geographical reach of the company.

The leaders from the Middle Eastern group clearly anticipated that the size of the deal for John's relatively small company would be so alluring that his neediness would soar and unnecessary compromises would inevitably follow. The foreign contingent requested large discounts and favorable terms across the board, including the exclusive use of the technology throughout the rest of the world—everywhere but the United States. As over-the-top as this and certain other demands were, such a deal would still have yielded a very lucrative agreement for John's company. The Middle Easterners understood this, and they thought the shortsighted perspective would overwhelm John, as it overwhelms so many businesspeople. They simply did not understand that John was steadfastly driven and guided by his mission and purpose, which emphasized the unparalleled benefits of his equipment and the value of this equipment for the customers. Simply put, this air-conditioning unit was the best that money could buy and it was fairly priced, and the intellectual property rights were not for sale.

John would only accept offers commensurate with this M&P. No exceptions, no matter how tempting they might be, including this offer from the Middle Eastern group. So John said no to the other side's demands. When they responded with anger and renewed their demands, he said no again—politely, of course. Two weeks later, he received a request for a meeting in the United States. Six weeks later, the Middle Eastern group agreed to John's terms. The deal was done, and the contract was large enough to transform John's privately held company into a very successful publicly traded company, which now provides its technology worldwide. Neediness did not drive John's decisions. Angry threats and demands did not faze him. That's the power of M&P. It requires you to sit back, take a deep breath, and think deeply not only about each negotiation but also about your entire business. My new clients benefit greatly just from the exercise of clarifying exactly what they are and what they want to do and what they must do.

Adhering to your M&P can be costly in the short run, which is why some people go off-track when the going gets tough. How many decisions make things tougher today but will benefit you dramatically in the long term? An excellent example is provided by Boeing's new policies. This story caught my attention by way of a headline in the November 28, 2006, *New York Times:* "Boeing Not Afraid to Say 'Sold Out.'" The story began, "Saying no to one of your best customers may not seem like a smart business strategy. But that is exactly what Boeing said this year to Southwest Airlines." Boeing has decided it's not going to repeat the mistakes of the late 1990s, when its sales force sold more planes than its production line could reliably produce. Write-offs to the tune of $4 billion followed. Executives were shown the door. Twenty thousand employees lost their jobs. Profits, stock price, everything plunged. But never again. Scott Carson, the chief executive of Boeing Commercial Aviation, said in the *Times* story, "In this hot market, it would be easy to be consumed with the desire to sell anything to people walking through the door who want to buy and push our production system to the point where you could break it. It's much harder to say, 'I'm sorry, we're sold out.'"

Imagine the internal conflict that preceded this decision to say no to Boeing's biggest customer. Apparently the new Boeing is determined to stay disciplined with its mission and purpose, which the company now realizes must emphasize the dependable execution of all sales. Scott Carson added in the *Times* report, "Frankly, we are much more disciplined than in 1997 and 1998. The message is, Don't get ahead of yourself; don't go crazy about how we ramp up." In the long run, Boeing, Southwest, and all the other customers will benefit from this strict adherence to mission and purpose—an adherence that virtually dictated the "no" to Southwest.

Bien, a pediatric nurse who came to America with her parents at the end of the Vietnam War to escape the chaos under Communism, wants to help stamp out sudden infant death syndrome and has invented clothing with temperature-sensing devices that help monitor temperature while a baby sleeps. This mechanism provides a quick and easy reference for any adult caring for the baby. It is a wonderful invention, but Bien has a problem. She can go to the market immediately and start earning a profit on her work, or she can apply for the patent that will protect her rights to her work. She will almost certainly need this protection, but the patent application is complicated and it will cost her entire life's savings. Nor will there be a decision for at least three years—perhaps five. Plenty of good people would "take the money and run" and hope for the best when the sharks start chomping away at their intellectual property rights. But Bien had developed a mission and purpose, and a vital part of this M&P was her *long-term* aim and her *continuing* responsibility. How, then, could she leave her invention unprotected? She couldn't. It was mission and purpose that gave her the conviction and the patience to wait until her patent was approved.

I've mentioned the company saddled with the terrible contract under which every unit was shipped at a considerable loss—and production costs were not the problem. (In my experience, they seldom are. The culprit is usually a team of negotiators taken to the cleaners by the customer.) The CEO of this particular company in trouble called the CEO of the other company and said, "We did a terrible job negotiating with you. You probably knew that at the time. I didn't. Now I do. How can we fix this?" I provided this story as an example of a CEO who decided to say no. Now I add the vital point that it was his M&P that gave him the conviction to do so.

Of course, developing the M&P was the first step for the entire renegotiation. An early candidate: *Become profitable again?* Not good enough. Everyone did want the company to become profitable again, but the more basic problem and issue was a lax negotiating culture that had to change if the company was to survive. *An entirely revamped outlook* would be the benefit delivered to this company's customer in this renegotiation. Consider this resulting M&P:

> To help [the other company's] top management see our company as a new and revitalized organization that is going to change its effectiveness to the benefit of their company and the whole industry, by becoming an effective supplier to that industry.

With such a mission and purpose, could the company continue to lose money on every shipment? No, because losing money on every shipment is not the hallmark of a revitalized organization. I'd call it the hallmark of a company that will go out of business sooner or later. I mentioned in the early discussion of this story that some seasoned negotiators are amazed at the audacity behind that phone call. But they're wrong, for the simple reason that the call was in perfect alignment with the new, valid mission and purpose. With that M&P in hand, it was easy for the CEO of this company to tell the CEO of the other company, "We were terrible negotiators. Now we're not. Let's go to work."

For a realtor working with buyers, the mission and purpose might be to help the seller see that it is in *her* best long-term interest that she accept this offer that she is able to secure from you today, because this really is a hot property. With that mission and purpose in hand, would you try to close the deal as fast as you can, or would you *invite* her to say no? As a commercial plumber, your mission and purpose might be to help the general contractors see that you bring great benefit to their projects by providing professional workmanship, using the highest-quality supplies and materials available, and guaranteeing on-time completion. With this mission and purpose in hand, would you buy inferior supplies and try to pass them on to those general contractors at the price of higher-quality plumbing supplies? As a travel agent up against all the travel sites on the Web, you might want your mission and purpose to help travelers see that your knowledge and experience in the field and your attention to details would enhance every aspect of their business and personal travel. With that mission and purpose in hand, would you spend all your time with a new customer bad-mouthing the websites or would you acknowledge their wonderful utility for *cost-conscious* travelers as you point out their complete inability to offer hands-on service?

Almost every week someone asks me if mission and purpose will work with kids. Yes, it will, and my own kids will agree.

Jim was our first. (I have three other sons and one daughter.) Jim hated spelling and didn't understand why it mattered—the old "but you know what I mean" argument. He was about nine years old when this started, and I decided it was time to at least try to entice him to proceed in a more mature fashion. One day, in my calm, fatherly way, I asked Jim to sit beside me so we could talk. The conversation went something like this:

"Okay," I said, "let's look at this, Jimbo. I'll ask a few questions and you think about them before you answer. Fair?"

"Sure, Dad, that's fair."

"Okay, what do you want to be someday? You can change your mind anytime, but take a peek today. You can be anything you want. What would you like to be?"

"Gee, anything?" Yes, anything. "Gee, Dad, I hadn't thought about it."

"That's okay, but give it a shot now. You can pick anything."

"Well, I don't think I want to be a pilot like you. Maybe a baseball player."

"Okay, good. Now, if it turns out you're not good enough to be a professional baseball player—you're very talented, but you know how hard the competition is—or if you get hurt and can't play professionally, what would you like to do?"

"Gosh, Dad, this is hard."

"No problem, take your time. What do you think would be fun?"

"Well, maybe I could teach and coach baseball, if I couldn't play."

"Good. Now, *as a teacher*—not as a student like you are now, but as a coach and teacher—how would you like to be perceived by other teachers, parents, and students? How important would it be that they respect you?"

"Sure, I'd want their respect."

"Okay, on what basis would they do that? On what basis do people arrive at their conclusions about you? When you don't even take the trouble to spell correctly, what will they conclude? They may say, 'Where does this guy come from? What kind of education does he have? How did he get this job? Does he realize he can't spell, or does he just not care? This is the guy who's teaching and coaching my kids?' "

I paused. Jim was quiet. I said, "You see what I mean?"

I know, it's tough to get kids to look at the long term, but with your help they can do it. Initially, you may feel as if you're grasping at straws in this process, and maybe you are, but tell me this: Would you be better off just sitting down with kids with *no* plan, *no* overview? Would such a wing-and-prayer approach prepare you for the barrage of challenges they will almost certainly throw at you? No way.

Basically, I was getting into my son's world and negotiating with him in order to influence him to write a mission and purpose for his education. Over time, Jim and the other kids developed the ability to list the features of something they wanted to do and the benefits of doing it. They learned to prioritize and come up with a mission and purpose. In those early days, I probably wasn't yet thinking in those exact mission-and-purpose terms, but the seeds were there, for sure. Both my kids and I were developing the Camp family thinking about mission and purpose. I even gave them every opportunity to say no—and they took full advantage of this opportunity, of course. *No, Dad, I don't like it this way.* So it's back to work. I've seen my own kids actually enjoy the process. Negotiating mission and purpose with your kids can provide real eureka moments of self-worth and self-guidance for them, and such moments have the secondary benefit of bolstering Mom and Dad. Because Jim wrote his own mission and purpose for his own education, he learned to spell, if a bit grudgingly. In the end, in high school he was elected to the National Honor Society and proceeded to Carnegie Mellon University. Not long ago he completed fifty missions in Iraq as an aircraft commander (so he ended up as a pilot, not a professional baseball player after all).

What happens when you have no solid mission and purpose to guide you? I began this book by introducing my friend Ralph, the real estate developer who ran into the stone wall at the local council many years ago. As we delved into the matter, his basic problem became obvious: He didn't have a valid mission and purpose, one that was rooted in the world of that council. He hadn't carefully analyzed the benefits his development would bring them and their community—a greatly enhanced tax base, for one, which would in turn help the beleaguered schools—and he hadn't begun to think about the ongoing tasks required on his part to deliver these benefits to the city and the council. When he did, he made progress. His vision of his own work as a developer was greatly enhanced, and by constantly returning to his mission and purpose, he was able to help the council see what could be accomplished and the track to making it happen.

In this day and age of "teamwork" in the business world, an agreed-upon mission and purpose for the specific negotiation is absolutely mandatory. Otherwise, chaos rules. Our coach Todd sat in on a complex, three-day negotiation involving one of our new clients, a Fortune 200 team that hadn't even started its official training with us. For three days, Todd said nothing. He just watched and took extensive notes as this truly world-class *(in theory)* negotiation team of a dozen members fell apart before his eyes. They were stepping all over and hurting one another in every imaginable way. The primary problem was the absence of an M&P that *all* team members had worked on, understood, and approved. These men and women had all the talent and brainpower in the world, but no system to guide their actions, behaviors, and decisions. No cohesion. No mission and purpose.

Who would believe a *CEO* would sabotage his own company's negotiations in the same witless way? Well, it happens more often than you might think with chiefs who are not in close touch with the negotiation, have no understanding of the team's M&P, and therefore are vulnerable to bad decisions (much more vulnerable than their employees on the team). I was once coaching a Bendix team in a long and involved negotiation. It was moving forward on many fronts, but we were miles apart on the discount the other side wanted. The CEO of the other side called the Bendix CEO, who almost instantly agreed to an 18 percent discount. He never consulted his own negotiating team. He was ignorant of their M&P. He made a ridiculous, *needy* decision.

Let's return to that consummate inventor Thomas Edison, with the subject this time not the ticker-tape machine that he invented but the lightbulb. He did not invent the bulb. He developed it. It was clear to him that without the lightbulb, humanity would have trouble seeing how electricity could change humankind. I don't think Edison was armed with the authoritative M&P I urge you to develop, but he certainly had the equivalent. In the early ages of R&D, when no one else "saw the light," he invested thousands of his own dollars in the new invention, buying the rights and patents and hiring the inventor, English physicist Joseph Swan, to work with him to perfect the thing. Edison spent his own money to install dynamos in a New York neighborhood and to wire an entire city block so that the inhabitants could see how electricity could improve their lives. What was Edison's company? General Electric. What was its slogan? "We bring good things to life." There's a slogan with the attributes of a valid M&P implicit within it—ongoing responsibility and focus on the world of the other side, the customers.

As a coach, I see people waste a great deal of energy and time on issues and questions that just don't matter.

"Did I get as much as I could?"

"Should I have done better?"

"How much did I leave on the table?"

"I hope I wasn't too strong."

"I hope I wasn't too easy."

I could extend this list for pages. So could you, but soon you will be able to forget all such needless worries. With mission and purpose, you will not be sidetracked by the million little quibbles that can start gnawing at your mind and your emotions. This freedom will liberate you in a negotiation. You won't waste a moment debating with yourself whether this agreement you are about to sign or have just signed is win-win, win-lose, lose-win, or lose-lose, because such *scorekeeping* is suddenly seen for what it is: arbitrary and meaningless. You don't have to worry about whether you *get* every last dollar out of the deal or whether you *give* enough dollars to make the deal. Both of us hope you do receive the very last dollar and give up the fewest dollars, but this hope can never be resolved. *Could that 18 percent discount have been 19 percent?* As the buyer, you'll drive yourself crazy thinking like that. *Seventeen percent?* As the seller, you'll drive yourself crazy thinking like that. All you want to know is that the 18 percent, given or received, satisfies your mission and purpose.

Over time and with diligent application, you will learn how to identify your mission and purpose. As you set these guiding lights in place, you may discover a great deal about yourself, your business, and even your life as a whole. When the pieces do come together, the clarity will completely transform every negotiation.

Three-Minute Checklist

- Is your mission and purpose in place for this negotiation, this meeting, this conversation? If not, stop. Go no further. Prepare one.
- If the mission-and-purpose statement is in hand, read it. Absorb it. If necessary, have it handy for quick consultation.
- Are you emotionally and mentally prepared to let the mission and purpose guide your every move? If not, stop. If necessary, cancel the meeting or don't make the phone call.

5

How I Got My Boat

How Vision Drives Decisions

The people on the other side are negotiating for their benefit, not for yours. This is self-evident but often overlooked, and it's the reason your mission and purpose must be rooted in the world of the other side and bring benefits that solve *their* problems. Likewise, the other side is making decisions based on their own perspective, not on yours. What counts in the end is what *they* see, and what they must see is the benefits you bring to the negotiation.

> **Mission and purpose creates, guides, and enhances *vision*. The vision of the other side drives the effective decision-making that leads to agreements.**

In fact, vision drives just about everything you do. Before you decide to buy anything, sell anything, or sign anything, you have to have a vision. No vision, no decision. Why do you want this house? This heart-shaped swimming pool? This boat? This dinner date? This agreement? This job? This college? Even this pair of socks? In each case, the answer is a vision of some sort. It may not be much of a vision, but there is one, even with the pair of socks. With the socks, maybe you see comfortable, warm feet, maybe blister-free feet, maybe stylish feet. Whatever. Vision drives your decision to buy this pair of socks and not that one.

My wife Patty is the love of my life, and she is very easy to please—if I can build her vision. This was one aspect of my mission and purpose in the negotiation with her to buy a boat for the family. I'd always wanted a cruising boat, but she wasn't so sure. I was thinking of a used boat to get us started, something nice but with a number attached to the purchase that would lower the risk in case we really didn't like boating and had to turn around and unload the thing. Patty agreed to look, and it soon became apparent that while I saw really nice boats, she saw *used* boats. I saw reasonably priced and low-risk boats; she saw used. I saw sturdy; she saw damaged goods. I saw fishing; she saw a dirty boat still stinking of old fish.

How far did we get in the used-boat negotiation? You know the answer. Patty wasn't even sure we should buy a boat at all, but in the negotiation for a used model her vision was bad, and her decision was no.

On the sly, I'd been doing my research on the Web for new boats. I had a pretty good handle on what was out there and for how much money, and I'd even picked out the exact model I wanted Patty to like. But I did not mention this, and I didn't show her any pictures of it. Instead, I bought a few boating magazines and left them around the house so she might pick one up and see a boat she liked. Quite simply, I was working to build her vision, to get her to see in her mind's eye what she might want. Sure enough, she started browsing through the magazines and saw two or three new models she thought were nice. One day she announced that if we were going to do this, we needed at least three bedrooms and two baths, a floating home large enough to take some of the kids and the grandkids with us on our expeditions. This was progress! Expensive progress! She was beginning to see *her boat!*

We went to the Cleveland Boat Show, but we didn't walk

around at random. I had routed a course, saving my choice for last. As I thought would be the case, she wasn't sold on any of the models we saw on the way. Then we stopped in front of my choice. Her first comment was, "I like the lines of this boat. I like the idea of being up high and looking down. From up there I bet you can see turtles and dolphins and fish. The kids would love that."

Her vision was getting clearer. As we took off our shoes and climbed aboard, we were drawn into the main cabin by the music from the terrific stereo system and by the soft lighting that gently highlighted the amenities throughout. The interior leather was tan, and the interior cabinets were cherry. I had to admit it was really nice. Patty commented, "Now this is more like it." The salesperson who showed us around explained that it would take about 120 days to build our boat to our specifications. Patty would have to go to the factory to work with the decorators. That invitation brought a smile to her face, and she said, "I could do that. I can see myself doing that. In fact, I deserve to do that." I laughed, because that was her favorite line when she really wanted something. As we continued through the boat, she actually said she could "see" Brian and Todd in this room, Kristi in this room, or James and Jordan in this room. In the end, we bought this boat, and it has brought our family hundreds of hours of pure enjoyment, and it would never have happened without Patty's vision, built over a period of months.

Test Drive Recall a recent purchase—or every recent purchase. What did you *see* before buying? What was your *vision?* You had one.

Test Drive Recall your most recent negotiation. Again, what was the vision that induced *them* to sign the agreement? What was your vision?

Make no mistake about it. The most gullible shopaholics won't buy a ten-cent trinket without some kind of vision of themselves or their children playing with this trinket, wearing

this trinket, using this trinket, or appearing to be special because of this trinket. If you have any doubt about this point,
please take a moment to think about it. Some vision in your
mind's eye is what leads you to buy *this* house, plant *this* flower,
negotiate *this* agreement. All of us make decisions based on a vision. No exceptions. It's just the way we function.

Why go to war? Why fight against someone? Why risk your
life to defend a way of life? Why pay these extra taxes? Why
support any important piece of legislation? In a representative
democracy, these questions are answered in a negotiation between the leaders and the people. In this political realm, you
could almost define leadership as the effective building of vision among the citizens by the leaders. What do the leaders
want us to see? If we share their vision, all is well and reelec-
tion is almost guaranteed. But if we do not share it, they're in
trouble. If we have a different vision, we show them the door
in the next election cycle.

"I see! Looks good to me! It's clear as a bell!"

"I can't see this! I'm blind to this! I'm in a fog!"

"They have to see this! How could they fail to see this?"

No vision, no action.
No vision, no decision.
No vision, no agreement.

When your M&P is rooted in the world of the other side, it
guides you in building their vision. Without that vision, they
will never take action. It's vital that you discover these two
principles for yourself and fully internalize them.

A VISION OF WHAT?

In negotiations, you must have a vision of a *current or future problem to be solved.* It's just that simple. This is why you're negotiating. Supplies and sales and inventory and overhead and profits are all problems that businesses face, in one way or another. The permutations are virtually infinite. In your daily life, the current or future problems you face with family, neighbors, and the businesses you deal with are definitely infinite. You make decisions and negotiate agreements in order to alleviate or otherwise address in some way this current or future problem you're facing. What else could any negotiation possibly concern?

Say you're the salesman for a machine confronted by a buyer who's in the market but fails to understand the importance of your specific machine. That's his problem in the negotiation: He needs not just any machine, but *yours.* This is not an unusual case in negotiation—you see the other side's problem before they do. As the salesman, your primary job is to build their vision of this technology as the future of the industry and of this machine as a dramatic competitive advantage. Without this machine on the shop floor, this customer will have a serious problem. You will never close this agreement unless you can build this vision. You want this buyer to have dreams about this machine. You want this buyer to see this machine leading the charge.

How do you do this? How do you tell someone, "You just don't get it" or "Folks, you've just wasted a lot of money on second-rate stuff"? For starters, you *don't* say, "You just don't get it" or "Folks, you've just wasted a lot of money on second-rate stuff. Mine is better." That won't get you anywhere. That just puts people on the defensive and destroys vision. Or maybe it does create one vision: their jobs down the tubes when they're fired for incompetence. This is not a good vision for them to have, because they'll fight it. Only with the most careful "painting" of the vision, as I put it, will they see your vision and accept it as their own vision. So you say something like this: "Now, I ask you to be patient with me here. Maybe I'm out of my mind. I want you to tell me if I am. Just say so. [This is the invitation to "no."] And everything I say is going to sound self-serving, I understand that, but with your permission, I'd like to describe what I see, and then let's look at it together to see if it makes sense to you."

Peter owned a company that facilitated data sharing from company to company—definitely a cutting-edge field, and very competitive. Peter met with Tim, a potential client he had met at a trade show whose company had been transferring data practically "by hand," copying it from Tim's own machine and delivering it to his users. Thousands of data records were literally being transferred by printing them out and giving the printed copies to the other parties. Tim didn't even know there was another way to do this, so Peter's first job in his follow-up was to create a vision for Tim of a problem he didn't even know he had. He doesn't do this by exclaiming, "You don't know about facilitated data sharing? Where've you been, Tim?" He does this by saying, "Let me show you what we do, Tim. It works beautifully for a lot of companies your size, but maybe it's not right for you. Let me know. Here goes. . . ."

Another story: William, a successful young entrepreneur, invested in a start-up in the late 1990s that provided server space for large websites. I asked William how he decided to take on this investment and to plunge into building his business. His answer was a textbook illustration of my point in this chapter. "Jim," he said, "from the moment I was introduced to the concept, I could see it. It was clear to me that here was the birth of a new industry. So we went about helping our clients see the possibilities about what we could bring to them through the Internet services we provide. They see it and it is a great business to be in. Our whole focus is their vision of what can be accomplished for them."

I didn't have a tape recorder with me, but that was William's answer in almost so many words. His business has now doubled in each of the last seven years. It's the industry leader by a huge amount.

In every negotiation, the vision of the problem and the solution is what brings the negotiators to agreements.

As the job applicant, you are head and shoulders above the field. This is a great advantage for you and a *problem* for the employer in the salary negotiation. You're perfect. They want you. They may even need you. This is the vision you want to build for them. Now turn it around. As the employer, maybe you're offering the opportunity of a lifetime for this applicant. If so, this is her problem in the salary negotiation. The money you offer isn't great, but the upside for the future is. That's the vision you want to build as you defend your offer. As a book editor, you've just read the manuscript for a terrific airport novel. From my perspective as the author's agent, the quality of this book is a big problem for you. You can't let it get away. I work hard to build your vision of this possibility.

In the discussion of neediness I noted that an auction may be the world's best mechanism for creating neediness in potential buyers. It's perfect for that purpose. I can now rephrase the lesson: The auction is tailor-made for building the bidders' vision of *losing* this purchase, this great airport novel. It is this vision that leads to the neediness that in turn leads to the offer you want.

THE TREASURE HUNT

You must strive to see clearly why the other party is really negotiating. What's their *real* problem? In many cases, the problem will be pretty straightforward and the issues pretty obvious. But sometimes you really have to dig, and sometimes a hidden problem you haven't discovered is subverting the entire negotiation. Acquisitions of any kind, from companies to houses to used cars, can be hotbeds of hidden problems. *Why are they so eager to close this deal? Why won't they give us the information we've asked for repeatedly? We must be missing something.* It's quite likely you are. Anyone with kids knows that the Monday morning stomachache probably is not the real reason Jane wants to stay home from school. Is it the unfinished homework assignment, the test she didn't study for, the argument she had with her best friend on Friday? Good luck finding out, and maybe it's not so important if you don't. But in business negotiations, you must.

You're bidding to become the new waste-management contractor for a large company. It's almost a given that someone or some clique in that company has a sweet relationship with the *current* waste-management contractor, and this individual or group of individuals may try to protect that relationship by subverting your negotiation. This is a big hidden problem for you. What if you sell life insurance? The likely customer might well tell the salesperson, "Well, I guess I just need some life insurance for my wife and kids." Okay, but such a diffuse problem and diffuse vision is probably not going to be good enough to close this deal. This customer needs a clearer and more *specific* vision of the problem, and it is the salesperson's job to help him or her find it. Maybe there is a specific health problem and accompanying vision of medical bills crippling the family. Or maybe there's the dream of a college education for the kids that seems unaffordable. Whatever the case, it will be the clear vision of the particular circumstance, not the general emotion, that generates the deal in the end. In any negotiation, it is always this *particular* vision of the real problem that will, ultimately, motivate the other side to make a decision.

When you face an apparently intractable problem in a negotiation, vision is almost certainly missing. The problem could be that you understand the problem on the other side and you have failed to build a vision of it, you have failed to uncover a problem that the members of the other side are actively hiding, you have failed to help those members of the other side see a problem they don't even realize they are hiding from themselves, or you have failed by avoiding their real problem because you're afraid it's just too tough.

Belatedly—several weeks after they had begun—I was brought into the negotiations between a Japanese firm and my client, Principa, an American company that provides and implements technical systems. The long and the short of it was that both sides were avoiding the real problem, but in different ways. The Japanese were playing all kinds of games with their claim that a work order rather than a contractual agreement would suffice for this agreement. Principa required a signed contract. A work order would not be sufficient. Yet the Principa negotiating team had been avoiding this basic problem for weeks, dreaming up all kinds of secondary issues and other problems rather than confronting the main one. Fear of losing the deal—that is, neediness—was driving their decisions. In the end, the real problem was addressed and the agreement was made.

Consider the saga of this acquisition negotiation that was already in progress when I was brought in by my client, Texi. The acquisition would be a nice fit, and if Texi could pick up the smaller company at the right price, excellent, but it was not an absolutely necessary purchase. There was no conceivable neediness on Texi's side—or at least there shouldn't have been. Before I arrived on the scene, unsolicited Texi offered $20 million and didn't get much of a response. In fact, they didn't hear anything. Then they learned that the sellers had hired an investment banker. To counter, Texi hired its own investment banker, and he had immediately put in a second offer of $30 million. The banker's idea (or assumption) was that this 50 percent increase would impress the sellers with Texi's enthusiasm and commitment for the deal, but the gambit didn't work. Now Texi was showing need—great need. They heard nothing, which was pretty frustrating, and they raised the price again. That's when Texi brought me in.

"What's your vision of their problem?" I asked the team leader.

"What do you mean?" he replied.

"What vision is driving them to sell?"

"Well, we think (assume) it must be [blah and blah and blah]."

"I see. Who have you been talking to over there?"

"Well, we haven't talked to them per se, but our banker talked to their banker, who said we'd have to do much better with our offer before they'd entertain it. [In short, the seller had said no.] So we upped our offer again to $43 million, this time with some stock."

"So is this where we are today?"

"Well, sort of. Our banker had said we should find out what they really wanted, so about five days ago I agreed and he asked them, and they said an offer would have to be seriously north of $50 million, with some stock, in order to be taken seriously."

Wow. The negotiating team had never talked with the sellers—not once. They had no solid idea why those folks were selling in the first place—no idea of the problem on the other side, that is. Since they didn't know the problem, they were therefore unable to build any vision on the other side. They had been told no three or four times and had raised their offer every time. All in all, not what I would have coached. Not what I would have coached in any way whatsoever! Who would make any offer at all without a full vision of what was going on with the other side? What was the problem on the other side? What did they want? What did they perhaps *need?*

The only people who would proceed so blindly are those who are seeking results over which they have no real control. Instead of working carefully with a system to set in place a valid mission and purpose, to identify benefits brought to the table, to identify problems on the other side, to build vision,

and to be prepared to say no, they were trying to manage a result over which they had no control. And they didn't understand this. They were just throwing numbers around — higher
numbers, always.

"Okay," I continued, "who are you bidding against?" The others in the room looked at me like I was the devil incarnate. The
team leader replied, "I've been doing this for twenty years and
I have never known who I was bidding against. That is not
something we do. That is too aggressive. I've never heard of
asking who we are competing against."

I said, "Well, what can happen if you do ask?" The answer is
that they can say no and refuse to tell you, or they can tell you.
So why not ask? You're not afraid to hear the "no," are you?

The leader's aide responded, "If we make them mad and offend them by asking, then they will really raise the price and it
will get really expensive." Wow, an amazing assumption rooted
in a fear of "no."

Wait a minute, I thought to myself. You're worried that
they'll get mad at you and raise the price, but you haven't even
spoken with them, so they can't be mad at you. Yet, you've already raised the price from $20 million to $50 million! I bit my
tongue, however, and we set about discovering what was really
going on and building vision. The real problem turned out to
be the desire of the owners of the privately held company to
keep it intact and in the same location. The other bidders had
exactly the opposite course of action in mind, breaking up the
divisions of the acquired company and moving them elsewhere, lock, stock, and barrel. Since Texi intended to keep the
company intact and in place, the job of building vision of the
problem for the other side went pretty smoothly. In the end,
the acquisition went through at about $50 million, and this
wasn't even the highest bid. The Texi team proclaimed to their
board and the public a great victory at a bargain price!

Maybe, but wouldn't it have been nice if the negotiators
had had full faith in a solid mission and purpose and had met
with the other side initially and uncovered the problem early

and built their vision of that problem? And wouldn't it have been more effective if the negotiators had been prepared to say no just once, or if they hadn't automatically responded to hearing no by raising their offer?

In fact, a wonderfully effective way to build vision for the other side is to ask them to tell you no. When that side carefully considers exactly what this "no" means or entails, their problem may become very clear indeed, and good things can happen for you.

> *Tell me if I'm wrong, Vince, but if my neighbors ask me about your work as a contractor and I tell them about the delays and what happened here—the truth—well, I don't think this would help you much in the future. What do you suggest can be done to correct this? How much business comes in these days from solid referrals?*

> *Mr. Jones, I know how important your son's education is for you. You've made it very clear and I appreciate your visit. Now I have an idea that I'd like you to think about and then make a decision on. Of course, you can reject this idea and we can maybe go in another direction, that's entirely up to you. But I would like to hear your thoughts on how important active support at home is for Johnny. What would twenty minutes a night working on his homework with you or Mrs. Jones do for his attitude? I've seen the beneficial effect of just twenty minutes many times with other children. What do you think?*

On the other hand, just about the poorest way to build vision is with early compromise. When Texi jacked up its price almost instantly—in effect, a compromise for no reason at all—it only undermined whatever vision the other side might have had. *Here Texi is raising its price already!* That's what they're thinking. *Texi must be the party with the big problem here! Texi must really need us!*

YOU DO NOT *CREATE* THE PROBLEM

I hope it's understood that I'm not talking about *creating* the problem for the other side. Many times I've heard someone say, "Boy, did I put them in some pain." That's ridiculous. You help create the vision of the problem, but you don't create the problem itself at all. It is already there. The doctor doesn't create your illness before prescribing treatment; she helps you see your case clearly.

Not even the retail salesperson is "starting from scratch." My wife and I didn't go to the boat show by accident. No salesperson in the world was going to be able to convince us that we had an aching need we didn't really have for that big boat. Likewise, no one wanders into an appliance store to buy carpet. They may not be ready to buy a new washer-dryer combination, but they want to *see* one. The salesperson always has something to work with. So, please, whatever the nature of your negotiation, forget any idea you may have about *creating* problems for the other negotiators. That's amateur hour. What you help to create is their *vision* of their very real problem.

I've been asked many times, "If I figure out their big problem and they don't, doesn't this put me one up? Doesn't it allow me to sneak up on them?" No, this is poppycock. It's not real-world. If the folks on the other side of the table don't see the real reason they need to finish your remodeling job on time or buy your widget or hire you as their consultant, what's their incentive in this negotiation? If they don't understand their own problem and don't have a vision that you can solve that problem for them, they'll never come to an agreement.

YOU CANNOT *TELL* ANYONE ANYTHING

Many people make the fatal mistake of thinking they can use their gift of gab or their nifty PowerPoint presentation or both to *convince* the other party with facts and figures to make the rational decision. These negotiators try to make the other side *understand.* But what's the problem with trying to convince someone to understand what you understand, to know what you know? To begin with, you're asking the other folks to come into *your* world. And where do you want to spend your time in a negotiation? In their world, of course. Second, you're forgetting the power of emotions in the decision-making process. You need the facts, of course, but the *context* in which those facts are being considered is the emotions. In the beginning and all the way to the end, decisions are made with your emotions, your gut, not with your head. This is why you cannot make the other side rationally *understand* and why you don't even want them to, not at first. You want them to *see* on their own. You cannot pound the facts into their brains. This only *inhibits* vision. The intellectual information just throws a wet blanket on vision. It puts people into an analytical mode. You would be better off not talking at all than pounding away with all your facts and figures.

> **There is a crucial difference between seeing and understanding, and seeing must come first. We must see in a visceral way before we can understand in a rational way.**

Classic example: the Thomas Edison story (see pages 23–24), in which the great man said not a word after he flipped the switch on his newest invention, the ticker-tape machine. He could have lectured for half an hour about its attributes, but Edison, genius that he was, and in league with his sidekick, the sage Colonel, understood that the best way to get the in-

vestor to see the value, the best way to build the investor's vision of that value, was simply to let this remarkable device run
on its own. Then he could explain how the contraption
worked.

To put this principle to the test, a very talented client
named Roger devised a clever experiment for his presentation
to a financial analyst. He made the presentation twice, once in
the standard didactic way, making point after point—all of
them good points—then a second time when all he did was
ask questions of the analyst. What can be expected by way of
ROI (return on investment) in this industry? What do you see
as a standard or benchmark in the area of growth? How many
opportunities should make up a quarter? And many more. In
the first presentation, the analyst sat quietly and took a few
notes. The second time he filled page after page with notes as
he enthusiastically engaged the analyst with the questions.
Since that day, Roger has understood completely the power of
asking questions as a way of painting the vision for the other
side, helping them see the issues for themselves.

If your idea is to try to convince someone to buy this product or service or to sign this deal, if your idea is try to *reason*
with the other side, you are setting yourself up for a difficult
career in negotiation and a difficult time dealing with people
in general. Instead, in all instances, you have to paint the picture that builds a vision that the other side can clearly see. A
key way to do this—the simplest, safest way to do this—is to
ask good questions. This is the subject of the following chapter, but I want to look quickly ahead with a wonderful story
that illustrates how just one or two simple questions or the
right kind of statements can sometimes create that vision and
quickly drive a decision. It also has a nice twist at the end.

A friend and colleague—a veteran businessman and an excellent negotiator—was the proud and happy father of a premature baby girl born with a defective heart valve, a condition
that's pretty common in preemies. Sometimes this valve can be
induced to heal with drugs, but if not, surgery is required. In

the case of Bob's baby, the drugs failed. Her doctors then wanted to move her to another hospital for the required surgery, the hospital where the best pediatric thoracic surgeons practiced. Bob and his wife saw no reason for this move. They feared that transferring their daughter to another hospital was too much of a risk to take, especially since their hospital had a state-of-the-art neonatal unit with an operating theater attached. A meeting with the doctor in charge of the neonatal unit was scheduled. This was a negotiation, wasn't it? Yes, and Bob understood the necessity of keeping his emotions in check in order to prevent the doctor from lumping him and his wife—understandably, perhaps—into the category of emotionally overwrought parents who don't have to be taken seriously on matters of treatment. So Bob had to build a lot of vision with very few words.

He asked this single question: How much risk are you willing to take with my child's life? That question was designed to get the doctor to ask that question of himself, in his own world: *How much risk am I willing to take to transfer this young couple's precious baby?* The doctor considered his answer carefully. To his great credit, he did not shoot from the hip, know-it-all-style. (Some doctors are prone to that, but then so are many other people.) And though he knew nothing about my principles of negotiating, he intuitively understood that in the previous conversations with these parents he had not painted a clear enough picture to allow them to see *their* problem. So he replied to my friend's question by saying, "Yes, there is a risk in transferring your baby to another hospital and there is an excellent operating theater at this hospital; we could request the specialists from the other hospital to come over here. But, the *real* risk here is not during the operation but later—post-op complications. If the baby is moved to the other hospital, she will have the best care available to her within seconds if an emergency arises after the operation. If she remains here, the best care will be an ambulance trip away."

This was a really efficient negotiation in which *both* parties worked to clarify the vision on the other side of the table—the best of all situations, a real decision-driver. As a result, the parents immediately changed their minds and made the decision to transfer their daughter to the other hospital. The operation was successful, post-op complications were minimal, and the baby is now a perfectly healthy youngster.

**The *clearer* the vision of the problem,
the *easier* the decision-making process.**

Or think about it this way: If your electrician doesn't paint for you a crystal-clear picture of the problem with your electrical circuitry, will he ever be able to convince you of the necessity of tearing out the walls and rewiring everything? Somehow I rather doubt it. The same psychology pertains to any negotiation. The folks on the other side have got to *see* for themselves.

As I emphasized earlier, adhering to your mission and purpose will keep you from going seriously astray in a *negative* direction—from making decisions that are detrimental to your mission and purpose and the negotiation. Building vision gives you a tool for keeping oriented in a *positive* direction. If things seem stalled out, pursue vision. The attempt will never hurt you.

Lack of vision on the other side is never their fault. Don't blame them. Look to your own work and ask yourself how you can do better in building their vision and moving the negotiation forward. If you are convinced you have done your best work and they simply have no vision of their problem, no vision of why they need this agreement—and this is sometimes the case, of course; plenty of healthy young people simply cannot be seduced into seeing their need for health insurance—it might be time to offer a friendly handshake and say farewell. Vision is that important. If you just can't build it, you're wasting your time in the negotiation.

Three-Minute Checklist

- Are you certain you clearly see the problems on the other side? Are you clear in your mind how to build the other side's vision?
- Are you clear that they have to *see* before they can understand?
- Are you ready to put aside the facts and the figures, because you cannot tell anyone anything?
- Are you ready to ask questions in order to build vision, rather than provide answers?

6

Socrates Has Nothing on You

The Art and Science of Asking Great Questions

So how do you get the other side to see for themselves what their essential problem is? How do you build their vision? How do you get them to see what you see without *telling* them what you see? How do you correct misunderstandings? How do you stop people from hedging, fudging, saying maybe, maybe, maybe, and even outright lying to you? How do you come to agreements that stick?

The safest way is with questions. A small subject? Hardly. Long experience has led me to emphasize the power of good questions to turn on the vision for the other side.

> **Questions are a key way we can peel the onion and find out what's really going on with the other side—find out their real problems, and then build their vision of those problems.**

You probably haven't noted that I've accentuated my points in the preceding chapters by posing questions that invite your consideration. My plan has been simple: I'm trying to solve the problem all coaches in any field have, which is to help their clients—the readers of this book, in my case now—create their own vision of the principles and practices the coaches hope to instill. There is no better way to do this than with a good question that engages the client and builds vision. Recall my friend and colleague Bob, the father of the premature baby. When I asked him which element of my system had the most immediate beneficial impact on his work, he didn't say the caution against neediness, mission and purpose, or "no." Those placed two, three, and four for him. First was asking good questions. In his negotiation with the neonatal doctor regarding the question of transferring his daughter to another hospital, Bob was so concerned about controlling his emotions that he relied on the one carefully chosen question to build vision: "How much risk are you willing to take with my child's life?"

I've told the story about Thomas Edison and the Colonel building the vision of the prospective buyer of the ticker-tape machine by simply turning the thing on. Its value was so self-evident that words were unnecessary, but if words had been necessary, one simple question from Edison would probably have done the trick: *How do you think you could use this device, sir?* The banker would have had to generate his own vision in order to answer that question.

Good questions can be as magical as Edison's new machine, but many people come to negotiations saddled with the burden of having to be the smartest person in the room. That's how they've lived their entire lives, beginning in grade school, and the way they've accomplished this (in their own minds) is by correctly *answering* questions—often before the question is even asked—by talking all the time, informing, expounding, explaining, teaching, pontificating. The longer they go on, the worse it gets. Very few people are trained to *ask* questions and listen carefully to the answers, and even those whose professional work depends on this skill—I'm thinking of doctors now—often don't do a very good job of it. Some do, of course; many don't. They can be so constrained by time and bureaucratic formulas, and so dependent on laboratory tests, that they forfeit one of their key diagnostic tools: good questions. I've had firsthand experience. My mom was a brittle diabetic and lived to be almost eighty years old. When she suffered a heart attack, we rushed her to the hospital and she was immediately put into intensive care. The doctor started his assessment of the situation by asking my dad and me what had happened. He then immediately began treating her cardiac condition. So far, so good. But he failed to ask if there were any other complicating factors in my mother's medical history that he should know about. He didn't really want to listen when we tried to tell him about her diabetes, but we forced him, because we were afraid she'd go into diabetic shock.

I've had equivalent firsthand experience with lawyers—and I don't mean in the courtroom, where the exchanges are tightly controlled by rules. I mean in depositions, where the parties can take more liberties, and in attorney-client consultations in the office. The lawyers usually did get around to asking the right questions, but often not in the best way, and often after a good deal of fumbling around. Frankly, I doubt that the efficient question-and-answer exchanges we enjoy on television are the rule. In my experience, they're not.

In the best-case scenario, the doctor and the lawyer are trying to find out as much as possible about the issues of the case. So is the negotiator. In this role, you must *inhabit* the world of the other side, because that's where their decisions will come from, by definition. You do this by asking good questions about that world and working hard to see it as they see it. Once you see what they're seeing *right now,* you ask more good questions to build their vision of what they need to see to move the negotiation forward.

How do you think you could use this widget on your production line, Mr. Jones?

**The other party's answers to your questions
build the vision that they need
in order to make the effective decisions
that drive the negotiation.**

Your questions also serve the further beneficial purpose of helping you control your own neediness. A question that might seem a tad naïve may even help you be a bit un-okay.

GETTING GOOD ANSWERS

Asking questions is a science and an art. The science is found in how you construct your question. The art is found in your tone of voice, your body language, and your remarks before asking your questions. So now we're going to get pretty technical, and we have to, because technique is everything here.

First, the "science." In the construction of your questions, you can begin with a verb or with an interrogative. The verb-led question is just that, a question that begins with a verb.

Should *you do this?*

Is *this what you want?*

Can *you accomplish this?*

Do *you need this?*

Will *you have authority to do this?*

Do *you have 5 minutes to see me?*

There are three possible answers to these questions: "yes," "no," and "maybe."

Yes, *I should do this.*

No, *this isn't what I want.*

Maybe *I can accomplish this.*

Yes, *I need this.*

No, *I don't have this authority.*

Maybe *I have 5 minutes to see you.*

In the discussion of the "no" principle in Chapter 3, I laid out in detail why "maybe" is a worthless answer that gives you nothing to work with. It muddies the water. It wastes time. It may even kick up some emotions that you don't want. *She said "maybe," but did she really mean "yes"? Maybe we're almost there!* And "yes" itself is real double-edged sword. *Yes, Ralph, I do need this. Just give me a call next week. I need to check with the boss.* Such a "yes" is worthless. Or recall this scenario from Chapter 3:

"John, will you straighten up your room? Your grandparents are coming for dinner."

"Sure, Mom. Don't worry."

Like the first "yes," this one means squat. It's just another word to deploy at the right time. There are a million ways and reasons to say yes but not really mean yes. Since "yes" is dicey and since "maybe" is inherently worthless, you're left with "no" as the only answer to a verb-led question that stands a pretty good chance of really telling you something. With only one worthwhile answer out of three possibilities, it follows that verb-led questions are risky at best and often just a waste of time. That's one problem with them.

Another problem is that verb-led questions often seem to people as if you're driving for a "yes." *Can you accomplish this?* This question seems to be calculated to take away the right to answer no. It seems subtly manipulative, and usually it *is* subtly manipulative. Most people don't really want to say no in the first place, as we've discussed, so if your question makes it even harder for them to say no when that's what they want to say, you have created an uncomfortable, defensive atmosphere, and this does you no good at all. You only drive the other side to

react with tactical and defensive thinking in order to (they believe) protect themselves.

Consider the difference between these two questions:

"Is this what you really want?"

"Isn't this what you really want?"

I'm betting that one of them—the second one—threw you
instinctively into the defensive mode. The inclusion of the one
little word "not" makes it a truly terrible question, because it in-
sinuates a "rush to close." Remember, no closing. Sooner or later
in the negotiation, the attempt will backfire. Sooner or later the
other party will react to your "Isn't this what you want?" question by saying to herself, "Thanks, but I believe *I'll* decide
whether this is what I really want. Don't push me."

Think about the courtroom grilling that is standard fare in
television dramas. The DA bores in with the questions: *Isn't it
true, Mr. Smithers, that on the night in question . . . ? Isn't it true that
you then unpacked your Smith & Wesson . . . ? Isn't it true that you then
climbed out the window . . . ?* Here's a lawyer who is intentionally
asking intimidating questions in an attempt to throw the wit-
ness onto the defensive, hoping for a Perry Mason–style break-
down and confession right on the stand. Sometimes it works, at
least on television. In a negotiation, *it never works.*

You're selling furniture at a garage sale and someone finally
comes up and asks about the overstuffed sofa with the shiny
spot in the middle of each cushion. You provide all necessary
information. You chat with this guy for twenty minutes. Your
patience is running thin. You blurt out, "Do you want to take
this sofa home? Can you say yes to this purchase?"

Yet another terrible verb-led question. As a direct result, you
can forget that sale. *Never* frame a question that seems to be
taking away the right to say no. You lose people, and you deserve to.

Okay, you're chastened by that debacle. You realize you have to try a different pitch with the next potential buyer. This time you blurt, "Is there any reason you wouldn't buy this sofa?"

This question is even worse than the preceding one, if that's possible. *Never* frame a question that might feel like an attempt to trick. Everyone reading this book would flinch hearing this question, and yet inexperienced negotiators ask these questions or the equivalent all the time. I'll admit that these scenarios here are rather tidy and not strictly real-world, all in the interest of making this point as clear as possible. Framing any question is very tricky and very important. You can blow a solid one-hour discussion or presentation in ten seconds with an ill-chosen, one-sentence question such as "Is there any reason you wouldn't say yes to this?" But it happens every second of the day, somewhere, because the ill-trained negotiator has been led to believe that he's *supposed* to ask such a question in order to push things along quickly.

Let's go back to the garage sale, this time to the table with the old stereo equipment. A collector saunters up and points at the eight-track.

"Does it still work?"

"You bet."

"Really?"

"Sure. I played *Rubber Soul* last night."

"Are you the only owner? Did you get it new?"

"Yeah, right here in town—the old stereo store that used to be on Elm."

The collector asks if he can pick up the eight-track. Of course. You then ask, "What else would you like to know?"

Now, this simple question is of a different sort altogether from those preceding ones. This question spawns some interesting dynamics. Mainly, it is a very comforting question for someone to hear. It demonstrates that you, the negotiator who has asked this question, have no off-putting neediness. I, the collector, feel okay, because you are at my service. You are certainly not closing, attempting to confuse me, or any of that negative stuff. Hearing this question, why would I have any reason to get defensive?

Just as important, this interrogative-led question does *not* have a quick answer. It *cannot* be answered with "yes," "no," or "maybe." The answer will necessarily be more extended than that. In my answer, I may provide some useful information, some emotion, some telltale waffling, or some insight. The odds are pretty good that my answer will contain *something* you can work with, because, as we know, people have a weakness for talking.

And who now has control in this conversation, you, who have asked the question "What else would you like to know?" and listened to the answer, or the collector, who's now doing the talking? You do. You, the *listener*. If you want to maintain maximum control—and you do, of course—let the other people talk as much as they want.

One remarkably powerful, simple question is this one: "What would you like me to do?"

Here, you invite the other side to indulge in what's likely to be a weakness for talking. The answer allows you to enter their world and their vision. You may well hear something like "Well, I need you to help me solve this problem," or "I'd like for you to fix this—that's what I'd like." Or you may hear a question in reply, one that may give you a world of information and that may even lay out the whole problem on the other side: "Well, if you started today, how long would it take you to have it ready?"

"How long?" So the timing of the completion could be a problem!

Whose world are you entering when you ask, "Now, why did you invite me to this meeting?" Their world. And their response may be "Well, we hope your package can help us. We've really been struggling with our deliveries and routing structure. It's a serious issue."

Whose world are you entering when you ask, "What's the biggest challenge you face right now?" Their world: "Inventory control. The market is changing so fast. One week widgets seem to be in with the kids, the next week they won't touch them. I don't know what to do."

How's that for fast progress in the information-gathering department? Good questions deliver such results time and time again. It's amazing.

Now, have you noticed the main difference between these good questions and any of the previous bad questions? The good ones are led by an *interrogative,* not by a verb.

"Who," "what," "when," "where," "why," "how," and "which": These famous *interrogatives* are the safest questions in a negotiation.

The interrogative-led questions will paint vision that will move the negotiation forward without the pitfalls of verb-led questions. They don't challenge the other party. They don't put them on the defensive. They elicit information and build vision. You have to be diligent and careful with all questions— with every word you utter—but the verb-led questions are almost all downside, while interrogative-led questions are a key means of discovery. They elicit details. They ensure thoroughness. They help the other side as well as us see what hasn't been seen and understood before.

Consider the following set of verb-led questions juxtaposed with a corresponding set of interrogative-led questions. In every case, which is better?

"Is this the biggest issue we face?" versus "What is the biggest issue we face?"

"Isn't this the biggest issue we face?" versus "What is the biggest issue we face?"

"Is this proposal tight enough for you?" versus "How can I tighten this proposal for you?"

"Can we work on delivery dates tomorrow?" versus "When

can we work on delivery dates?" or "How important are delivery dates?" or "Where do delivery dates fit in?"

"Do you think we should bring Mary into the loop now?" versus "Where does Mary fit in?" or "When should we bring Mary into the loop?" or "How does Mary fit into the picture?"

"Is there anything else you need?" versus "What else do you need?"

"Do you like what you see?" versus "What are your thoughts?"

"Does it fit into your needs?" versus "How do you see it? How does it fit for you?"

"Can you stay competitive without this machine?" versus "How can you stay competitive without this machine?"

"Do you want to look ridiculous?" versus "How would you like to appear to the outside world?" or "What advantages do you gain from studying?" or "What perception would you like to create for people?"

"Are you trying to make me angry?" versus "How do you want me to take that?" or "What does that accomplish?" or "How can we fix this and move forward?"

This rule about interrogative-led questions is not rocket science. Negotiators have been taught for decades to ask open-ended questions, and interrogative-led questions are simply one type of open-ended question. I emphasize the "interrogative-led" concept over the "open-ended" concept because I've found that it's easier to understand and to follow in the heat of a negotiation. Generally speaking, the negotiator who frames interrogative-led questions is on the right track.

Test Drive
Find a few family members or friends and ask them to play a quick game with you. Tell them you're going to ask some questions that might or might not seem

to follow one another logically. All you want them to do is close their eyes and raise a hand if they almost instantly "see" something—anything—in the mind's eye in response to each question. Make certain they understand that you're not testing them. Sometimes they may "see" an image quickly, sometimes they may not. Just be ready with the hands. Have your list of questions ready, most of them interrogative-led, but some verb-led. After each question, pause and make note of the raised hands. *Where* are you? *What* are you doing? *Is* the water blue? *What* color is the water? *How* high is the mountain? *When* was the last time you ate ice cream? *Do* you think we're going out to dinner? *Where* would you like to go out to dinner? I believe you will find that many more hands are raised in response to the interrogative-led questions. They induce people to see.

I've had many clients for whom this understanding was a *eureka* moment that took their negotiations to a whole new level very quickly. This was the case with Bob, the father of the premature baby. Do you recall the one question he asked the neonatal doctor in his effort to build vision: "*How* much risk are you willing to take with my child's life?" As we prepared for that negotiation, Bob and I did not believe that the doctor, or any other doctor, could hear that question without taking very careful stock of all aspects of the case—that is, without constructing the most complete vision possible of what could happen with this procedure. And that's all Bob and his wife wanted: a decision from the doctor based on the clearest possible vision. That's what they got.

Recall the question Thomas Edison and the Colonel could have asked the buyer of the ticker-tape machine if the demonstration by itself hadn't been enough: "*How* do you think you could use this device, sir?" Such questions build vision. The banker could not have answered the question without at least the first glimmer of a vision. A simple "How do I proceed?" can work wonders. The other folks will tell you! *How should I do this?* They'll tell you! *Why* do you think we're stuck on this point? They'll tell you!

Master questions and you'll understand how a successful negotiation really does take place in the world of the other side, not in your world. You'll understand the necessity of creating vision for the other side. And then a very strange and welcome phenomenon will follow: Your own neediness will fall away. You'll feel free as a bird in a negotiation.

Test Drive Prior to a meeting, jot the "big seven" interrogatives on your notepad. Who? What? When? Where? Why? How? Which? In this meeting, ask as many questions as possible with an interrogative. This exercise may seem mechanical at first—and it will be—but you will see how quickly the habit can be internalized and how effective these questions are.

KEEP IT SIMPLE

Keep your questions short. Anytime a question has more than eight or nine words, you risk complication. You may think that a long, compound question sounds impressive, but you're not in the business of sounding impressive, remember. Such a question serves only to kill vision and confuse people.

Another key is to ask *one question at a time.* Simple question by simple question, answer by answer, you will help the other side build their own picture of the issue. But negotiation is a very emotional arena, of course, and even skillful negotiators can get impatient and load one question on top of another, asking five or six in a row, barely pausing to take a breath, much less waiting for a thoughtful answer. Or you start off with a good interrogative-led question, only to answer it *for* the other person, or throw out a possible answer for her to consider. "What is the biggest challenge you face—is it the economy or your local labor problems?" This is one mistake (answering the question for her) followed by another mistake (turning a good interrogative-led question into a verb-led question). All we accomplish with this intervention is to impede the process of helping create vision.

So the rule is simple: You must take each question "slow and easy" and listen to each answer, because that answer is the clue for framing the next question.

> "What is our deadline for the project's completion?"

> "How critical is this September date for you?"

> "I'm not sure I understand. Why is September fifteenth so important?"

> "Oh, when did that problem with your deliveries begin?"

With such questions, be ready to take some notes, because you're about to learn something important.

BE CREATIVE AND PRECISE

Even interrogative-led questions have to be honed. You don't want to become mechanical and assume that since it's an interrogative-led question, it's the best question. It probably is a safe question, but this doesn't necessarily mean you can't do better. Be creative and consider the value of every word in the question. On this matter, I have a pet peeve that I'm convinced has validity beyond my own world. I believe trotting out the latest jargon in a question is mainly a good way to inhibit vision. Compare "How will you progress this issue internally?" with "How will you move this forward in your department?" With the first question, I can almost hear the grinding of gears in the brain on the other side of the table, and the culprit is the use of the word "progress" as a verb. With the simpler English of the second question, I hear the smooth engagement of the clutch. This question gives the other party an assignment in their world that may encourage or influence them to describe how they see themselves moving this forward. It's a little harder for them to see how they're going to *progress* this forward.

Compare these two questions:

"What is the approval process within Worldwide?"

"What are the steps for approval within Worldwide?"

If the approval process is complex, the first question poses a tall order for the other party—maybe too tall. The Worldwide folks may not know where to start. But the use of the word "steps" in the second question may help them break down the process within their own minds. They may at least see and tell you what the *next* step is, maybe even the next few steps.

Another comparison:

"What additional issues do you see?"

"What challenges have I missed?"

There's a subtle but potentially important difference here. With the first question, you're assuming that they're going to be trusting and open with you, and you thereby run the risk that they'll try to hide the real problem. The second question, substituting "challenges" for "issues" and putting the onus on yourself for failing to see something, is more likely to influence their vision and seduce them into telling you what they're really concerned about.

Tinker with your questions as you prepare for a meeting. Think about the impact of each word. Is this one or that one more likely to invite a free and open reply? (In the case of jargon, I vote for the other word.) Will it relax the other party, or put them on alert? Will it build their vision? Over time, I think you're going to come to my conclusion, that questions are fun. You won't be able to avoid the conclusion that they're definitely challenging—and very important. Believe it or not, some of my clients, including an automotive supply group, have contests for the best-developed and best-delivered question. The winners are treated to dinner by the other team members. Here are men and women who understand that their questions in negotiation really are an art, a science, and a necessary skill for succeeding at the highest level.

> **Don't get mechanical. Slow down, consult your mission and purpose, and think creatively about how to build the vision of the problem on the other side.**

AND DON'T FORGET TO NURTURE

According to family tradition, my great-grandfather used to say about the mules on his farm, "To get their attention you have to hit them between the eyes with a two-by-four. When you have their attention, they can see what they ought to do." But this doesn't usually work with us humans. It doesn't work at all in negotiations. We humans can be just as lacking in vision as mules, but we will not usually respond to the two-by-four. You want the people on the other side in the negotiation to see their problem clearly, but you don't build their vision of their problem by smacking them between the eyes. You soften the blow, so to speak, with nurturing.

The way you phrase questions and statements can be either nurturing or almost the opposite. Let's revisit some of the questions from the discussion so far and find the nurturing in them. *"Hey, how's it going?"* This is nurturing. *"That's a good question."* This is nurturing. *"Boy, you look grim."* Not quite so nurturing unless you're teasing a good friend. *"That question does nothing for me."* No nurturing here at all. *"How much did you invest in this piece of junk?"* An interrogative-led question, granted, but not one likely to build much vision on the other side. The "piece of junk" phrase ruins it. You'll have no problem identifying the nurturing element in the questions you ask and receive and no problem identifying the ones that come up short. Just be sure you subject your questions to this test.

The specific words you use are all-important. Also all-important for nurturing purposes is *how* you say them. *"How much did you invest in this 'technology?'"* Delivered sarcastically, this is not nurturing at all. The "piece of junk" *implication* hangs in the air. Delivered earnestly or naïvely or appreciatively, however, this question is definitely nurturing. Now think of the sentence *"Is this what you really want?"* It's somewhat dangerous in principle, because it's not interrogative-led, but these six words can cut either way, depending on delivery. If I say them abruptly and abrasively—"IS THIS WHAT YOU REALLY WANT?"—they're the opposite of nurturing. They'll get you nowhere. But if I ask the question quietly and with concern, even though it's a verb-led question, it's very nurturing. Delivery is everything. You instinctively know this, and some lucky individuals instinctively *do* this. I don't know about you, but I can still hear Ronald Reagan's natural, masterful nurturing, all of it accomplished with his carefully modulated tone of voice and that grandfatherly smile and shy dip of the head. Ronald Reagan was so good he was nurturing even as he pronounced the toughest words of his administration: *Mr. Gorbachev, tear down this wall!* The slow cadence was very important. Colin Powell is another natural with a commanding presence, literally, but he is also an instinctive nurturer. It's not easy to nurture while standing like a tower in an intimidating uniform glistening with medals, but he could do it. It's hard to resist that voice.

Quite simply, almost all of us prefer talking with and dealing with people who make us comfortable. Who are these people? Nurturers. Alas, most of us are not so naturally gifted in this regard as Ronald Reagan and Colin Powell. I know I'm not. I've had to spend my coaching career getting better, and I am getting better. You can get better, too.

Test Drive If you don't have a small tape recorder, acquire one, and record yourself while asking test questions and making test statements. You'll quickly understand the power of your delivery to affect the impact of your words. You can't miss the more nurturing delivery. Generally speaking, you'll see that a slower delivery and lower tone of voice have a beneficial impact.

And don't forget body language. When seated, relax and lean back. Avoid jerky movements. When they speak, calmly take notes. When you speak, slow your speech and lower your voice. If you're standing, lean against the wall, lower your posture. People are not going to deal effectively with you if you're towering and glowering over them. This is all common sense, but easy to forget in the heat of the moment.

Test Drive As you ask your test questions and make your test statements with the tape recorder in hand, adjust your body position and see how this position *alone* has an impact on your delivery. Your voice won't sound the same while you're standing straight and tall as it does when you're relaxing in a chair.

Nurturing is a key behavioral "goal" over which you do have control. It is the safety net that will always protect you in the highly emotional world of negotiation.

**The truly comfortable, confident negotiator
behaves like a nice person.**

I recently had a coaching session with Ron, the chairman of a strong Midwestern company. He was engaged in a very contentious battle with an auto manufacturer whose negotiation team was of the almost abusive type. After several name-calling sessions, Ron and his team were ready to try something else. I suggested deliberate, almost blatant nurturing, and they returned to the table with the explicit goal of keeping their voices down, way down—so low the aggressive gang on the other side had to listen very closely. Ron's team would *not* be baited by the raised voices on the other side. They would speak softly with their body language as well. And just like that, this negotiation got rolling! Ron and his team were able to address the real issues and ask the tough questions that would move the negotiation along.

This was not a once-in-a-lifetime experience for me as a coach. I emphasize nurturing because I know it works, time and again. Your ability to nurture the men and women on the other side, to put them at ease, is the key to assuring them that you are listening and that you value what they have to say. Nurturing is also just another way to allow them to feel okay.

Test Drive Pick a meeting, almost any meeting. The stature of the participants isn't important, the subject isn't important. In this meeting, focus on your own body. If you feel some tension building, breathe deeply and lean back in your chair. Take it easy. Modulate your voice. After the meeting, consider the "results." You definitely did not lose anything with this focus on your own body language, and you may well feel you benefited. Next, elevate your effort by picking a more important meeting—an actual negotiation—and test your nurturing behavior. Again, nothing will be lost, I promise, and something may be gained. After another test drive or two, you'll definitely know that you have benefited. In time, you won't even have to think about this. Your confidence will guide your body—and vice versa.

Don't misunderstand me. I'm not into touchy-feely negotiations. Nurturing must not be confused with being easy and soft. Nurturing does not mean "saving" the other side. You're not saving anyone. Nurturing is simply a way to release just a little stress at the right moment. It may well be the only way to ease yourself into their world, to build their vision, to move the negotiation forward.

Consider this situation: You're convinced that a potential customer has taken a potentially fatal fork in the road. You have the means to help correct the mistake, but how in the world do you go about painting the vision of this terrible problem for the other side? Say the potential customer is a fairly small company that has invested a lot of its money in a losing cause. The decision-makers of this company need to change, and quickly, but they're going to be defensive about the money they've already spent. They're going to fight to remain okay. So you certainly can't say, "Folks, you've just wasted most of your capital budget and months of work by some good people. That's the bad news. The good news is that our technology can bail you out." That won't get you anywhere. That won't serve your mission and purpose, because such statements *destroy* vision rather than build it. Or put it this way: Without nurturing, the only vision the other negotiators will have is their jobs on the line. This is not a good vision for them to have, even though it might be correct, because they'll fight it. But with careful nurturing, you can make the same point in a way that builds vision. You can lead them to see and accept the merits of the vision they need, the vision that they have to move in another direction—your direction.

Instead of the direct confrontation, say something like this: "Now, I ask you to be patient with me here, Sarah, but I've got a real problem. Maybe I'm out of my mind. I need you to tell me if I am. Just say so. [This is the invitation to "no."] And everything I say is going to sound self-serving, I understand that, because I am trying to sell you our widgets, but with your permission, I'd like to describe what I see, and then I'm going to ask you what you see. [Interrogative-led question to come.] We'll look at it together to see if it makes sense to you."

And off you go. Sarah will listen to you. She may still get defensive, but with this nurturing preamble, you have a fighting chance. Nurturing has nothing to do with *soft* negotiating, everything to do with *smart* negotiating.

Consider these statements:

I'm telling you, Betty, that won't work.

Steve, you should listen to those who know.

James, too many people on your team sit there and don't pay enough attention to details.

Carol, you're making a big mistake, and you're going to fail.

Good luck with any of these approaches. But what if you nurture, while changing the harsh statements into interrogative-led questions?

Betty, just a thought, but how many times has that worked for you?

Steve, I was wondering, who might you get to help with this?

John, the devil is in the details. How much time can your team spend on the details?

Carol, mistakes can be great learning tools. How much would it help if you avoided an unnecessary mistake?

Now you have a chance to build some vision. Any idea that nurturing is soft negotiating, that it gets run over by tough negotiators, or that it contradicts the "no" principle could not be more mistaken. Nurturing is simply one of your tools of the trade—an invaluable one. It requires the delicate touch—perhaps just the one right word, facial expression, or gesture. How you nurture will require great practice, insight, and reflection. When the going gets tough in a negotiation, your biggest challenge will be to nurture despite everything else going on. I should put that in boldface capital letters—but I won't, because that wouldn't be very nurturing of me, would it?

Three-Minute Checklist

- Are you prepared with good interrogative-led questions? They are not a magic bullet, but they are the safest way to build vision on the other side, and they are less likely to destroy vision.

• Being a defensive negotiator does you no good at all. Therefore always nurture. Don't attack, don't challenge, don't browbeat—not with your words, not with your body language.

7

Power Tools

"3+," Stripping, and Not Presenting

"3+" (or "three-plus"), another important tool of the trade, is the ability to remain with a question until it is answered at least three times, or to repeat a statement at least three times. This is not an original idea. Anyone who's ever taken a speech class knows the old rule: Tell them what you're going to tell them, then tell them, and then tell them what you told them. One, two, *three* times. I first heard the equivalent of this rule many years ago from a friend in sales and quickly learned that his advice was good. I've added the "+" because I've found that even three times may not be enough. So I coach 3-*plus* times. The more critical the negotiation, the more repetitions over a longer period of time you may require in order to fix the agreed-upon point. As always in negotiation, you're extremely suspicious of "yes." In the early stages, it's usually worthless, and so you should assume. In the later stages, when you're nailing down points of agreement, 3+ing is mandatory in order to make as sure as possible that the "yes" really is a "yes." You can even announce that you intend to make an important point three times. Rarely if ever will you feel the need to, but doing so will never hurt you.

In practice, it's difficult to overdo the 3+. Almost impossible. *The problem is, Damion, I don't know if the timing on this is right. Perhaps it is, but I'm not sure. Is the timing right? I wonder.* That's four repetitions, each a little different from the others. Now recall the story about the company requesting renegotiation of a contract because of the poor negotiating of its previous team. The executive called his counterpart at the other company and laid out the situation in grim detail. He said, "We have failed as a supplier. We did such a poor job of negotiating with you that we can't deliver another machine. It's clear that we failed. I didn't realize it at the time, but we failed. We failed as a supplier. Thanks to that failure, we are stuck in a bad position and can't meet our commitments. We've let you down."

Five uses of the word "failure." Not too many.

Test Drive It couldn't be simpler. At your desk or driving in your car, consider a statement like "The problem is, I don't know if the timing is right" or a question like "When should this be done?" Now "play" with different ways to make the point three or more times. When you're comfortable with the general idea, pick a meeting, any meeting, and then pick a point you want to make or a question you want to ask and 3+ it. And don't forget a nurturing voice and demeanor. You will see that people do *not* resent being the object of 3+ing. They appreciate the clarity. They respect your diligence.

No point is too small for 3+ing. *Okay, Bill, see you at three on Monday.* Did Bill hear you clearly? Did he make the note on his calendar? You don't know for sure, but it's easy to improve your chances greatly: *Good, Bill, I'll see you at three on Monday. Are you sure that's good for you, three P.M. Monday? ... Okay, I have it down. Three o'clock Monday.*

On more substantive points in a negotiation, 3+ing is absolutely mandatory. *We need help with limiting our liability. If we fail on liability, we've really damaged any opportunity we have with this agreement. How can we help you see the importance of limiting the liability? Your agreement on liability will really push this over the top.*

Vital point: The 3+ principle cannot seem like pressure in any way. It cannot *be* pressure in any way. You cannot sound *needy* to nail down this point. You are not rushing to close three times. Just the opposite, in fact. You're asking for "no" three times! That's the way to think about it. Whether you employ 3+ or 20+, always allow the other party every opportunity to say no. Three-plus goes hand in hand with "never close." As I've discussed in several different contexts, you grant the other side every opportunity to think through the situation, look at it from different perspectives, see for themselves what their decision really means, then verify it or change it. Without such clear, vivid vision, there will be no real decisions that lead to agreements that stick.

Say you sell cars and a guy walks in and announces that he wants this incredible green car right now. You could say, "Great, I'll get the keys and the paperwork!" and maybe the sale will go through. The smarter, safer approach that will yield more sales that stick is to take a step back and find out what's going on here. Is this guy playing some kind of game, conducting an experiment for his graduate degree in marketing, or has he really done his due diligence on the Web and come to his decision, with you as the lucky beneficiary? You have no idea. So take that step back, lower your voice, and say, "Today? Wow. That was fast. You want this MTV700 *today*? Right now? This is a substantial investment. How do you want to pay? Do you want us to finance it?" With 3+, you can flush out the truth pretty easily and effectively.

THE POSITIVE STRIP LINE

See the pendulum swinging back and forth, back and forth, back and forth? So swing the emotions in many negotiations. Initially, the pendulum is probably stationary. Emotions are calm, neither positive nor negative. Then something happens, someone says something, and this remark pushes the pendulum toward the negative direction. Then some factor halts the movement toward the negative and pulls the pendulum all the way past neutral and toward the positive side. Some of these back-and-forth emotional swings may seem good for you at the time, but in fact most of them are detrimental to the negotiation, even catastrophic if they're big and dramatic.

> **The task of the good negotiator is to keep the pendulum as close as possible to a calm, "stationary" mode. The big negative swings don't do anyone any good in the long run, and neither do the big *positive* swings.**

Consider a straight sales situation, although the picture works just as well for any negotiation of any kind. If you allow your potential customer to swing too hard into the positive mode, what happens when the almost inevitable second thoughts and doubts set in? Well, the pendulum that was so high in the positive mode will probably swing down with so much momentum that it carries all the way through the neutral zone and into the *negative* zone. If this happens, what do you do? Maybe you recover, maybe you don't. The folks who helped my mother on her shopping sprees usually didn't. You see, Mom was famous for making spontaneous fashion purchases, then changing her mind the following day and taking the dress or the purse back. The eternal optimist might hope that yet another change of emotion would have returned Mom from deep in the negative to high in the positive again and she'd buy the dress after all. But that's not usually how it works in the real world. To my knowledge, the salesperson was *never* able to get Mom to change her mind again, and a lot of time and energy had been wasted. With her, buyer's remorse was final.

The big swings in sales or any negotiation are a vicious circle. If someone did succeed in getting Mom back in the strong positive mode, what would stop her from swinging harshly negative when she returned home the second time? Nothing. The big emotional swings are impossible for you to control— but you must maintain control, or at least try your best to do so. So what's the solution? It's simple (in theory): Steer the negotiation away from the emotional extremes, both the strongly negative *and* the strongly positive. Stay in the calm neutral range, which is where we find the good agreements. The salespeople dealing with my mom should have said something like "It's a beautiful dress, Mrs. Camp. But don't you think this orange is unusual? How about trying it on before you decide? ... Wow, it's beautiful. What do you think? What shoes might you have to wear with it?"

Of course, this is totally contrarian negotiating. *You mean I don't want them to get all excited?* No, you don't, because the excitement won't last. Most people are like my mother to some degree, and those inevitable second thoughts will come along sooner or later. The key is that you want the doubts to surface *sooner* rather than later, because you'll have a better chance of influencing those doubts, a better chance of keeping the situation closer to the calm, neutral zone. *But don't you think this orange is unusual? How about trying it on before you decide?* A gently flickering flame of interest is better than a raging bonfire. On the other hand, you don't want a pile of dead ashes. So throw neither gasoline nor foam on the fire. Instead, use the tools presented in this chapter.

Remember the car salesman (you) who 3+ed the guy who walked in and announced his intention to buy the green MTV700? You said, "Today? Wow. That was fast. You want this MTV700 *today*? Right now? This is a substantial investment. How do you want to pay? Do you want us to finance it?" That works fine. Or you could adopt this approach.

This is the one! I'll take it now!

Good choice. It's a beauty, but you know this green is difficult to keep clean.

*I don't care about that. I'll wash it every day
anyway or at least every few days.*

*This car definitely deserves that kind of care, but I
want to tell you that it's completely loaded with
every imaginable option. In fact, I think it's the most
expensive car in stock, bar none. I'd enjoy showing
you a few others just to help you be sure this is the
car for you.*

*Are any of them as nice as this with a few less
options?*

*Let's take a look. You be the judge. I just want to be
sure you get exactly what you want.*

Thanks. Let's look around.

You are one excellent salesman and negotiator. You have
skillfully maneuvered this fellow out of the wildly positive
mode and into a milder one that's much more likely to be productive. You're still not sure exactly what's going on here, but
you'll find out soon enough. Sure, you could have gone for
broke and whipped out the paperwork for the green MTV700,
but you have a system and you stay within it. You also know
that if this gung-ho guy really was going to buy the most expensive car on the spur of the moment, he'll still buy it half an
hour later. If he wasn't, maybe you have a chance with another
model. This is how you find out.

The term I use for this tool of the trade is "stripping line." It
comes from a fishing technique in which you do *not* set the
hook until you let the fish run off some line and burn up some
energy in the process. With certain fish, setting the hook immediately would put on too much pressure and rip the hook right
out. By letting the fish run, by stripping some line, you avoid
putting on too much pressure. Maybe that fishing analogy

speaks to you, maybe it doesn't, but stripping some line in negotiation definitely should interest you. It must interest you.

More specifically, the car salesman was using a *positive* strip line. You use this to put a damper on suspiciously positive emotions. In effect, you apply a *gentle brake* as a way to bring everyone back more toward a more neutral position from a position that's perhaps overly exuberant. You make a point that calms everyone down and invites the other side to pause for reflection. In the little story about my mom's ill-fated impulse purchases, I suggested that a salesperson would have been wise to say, "It's a beautiful dress, Mrs. Camp. But don't you think this orange is unusual? How about trying it on before you decide?" These gentle remarks were positive strip lines—the gentlest possible brakes that would have given Mom something to think about. She might have bought the orange dress anyway, only to return it the next day, but your chances of controlling the impulse, perhaps guiding it toward a purchase that had a better chance of sticking, would have been much better.

When I introduce this tool some people's first reaction is "You must be kidding." Hardly. It's then a lot of fun for me to see the initial doubt turn into enthusiastic endorsement, as they see how effective it is. Sometimes they get so excited I have to use a positive strip line to draw them back a little! It's not a panacea, just a darned good tool that works. And you're always safe with the positive strip line. As with 3+, it won't backfire. The only sale you'll lose will be the one you were going to lose anyway.

I now let my client Greg tell his own story:

> Mrs. Jones was in her late sixties, and she had just recently lost her husband. I had been introduced to her by another client, and in our first meeting Mrs. Jones told me how happy she was to have this recommendation from a close friend she trusted. I thanked her but added that we must be sure that we agree on any recommendation I made. This was an early invitation

for her to say no. [It was also the mildest possible positive strip line—the slightest tap on the brake.] Well, Mrs. Jones then said that she was sure that whatever I recommended would be just fine. I told her that I was and am proud of my work, but I could not in good conscience offer any advice for firm action without checking with her accountant or attorney. [Another tap on the brake.] She agreed, I made my recommendations, she approved them, I consulted with her accountant, and then I returned to Mrs. Jones with her new financial package. When she wrote a check for more than $330,000, I handed it back and asked her to be sure she was comfortable with the program. Did she have any doubts at all about the path we were on? [This was both an invitation to "no" and a perceptible tap on the brake.] She looked at me and said she was sure this was the right path and gave me the check. Two days later she asked me to come and speak with four of her widowed friends who needed help.

True story, and I could substitute literally hundreds. Greg himself could give you dozens more. The simple truth is that I could not name one instance in which a positive strip line has ever backfired for me or any client. It just doesn't backfire. To believe that it might is to misunderstand human nature and your purpose as a negotiator. To believe that it might is to be stuck in a "rush to close" mode.

The positive strip line also controls any neediness of your own, reinforces the right to say no, lets everyone feel okay, and gets you deals that stick.

Test Drive In a negotiation with low stakes, try a quiet positive strip line, something like "That's great, Joan. I appreciate your interest. Your enthusiasm is gratifying, but we still have a lot of challenges to work on." This will not backfire on you. Ever.

THE NEGATIVE STRIP LINE

Now consider the opposite scenario, in which the pendulum is too far to the other side—deep into negative, hostile territory. Here you use a *negative* strip line. With this tool, however, you do not try to brake the negativism. Instead, you are even *more negative.* That's right. By insinuating yourself right into the heart of the negativity, you startle the other side and thereby invite them to look at their attitude more carefully.

A wonderful example of the effective use of this tool is provided by the movie *Legal Eagles,* in which Robert Redford plays an experienced assistant district attorney who has just been fired for reasons too complicated to discuss here. He joins Debra Winger, a small-time defense attorney, in her advocacy on behalf of the Daryl Hannah character, a beautiful young woman accused of killing her lover. This is a dream case for the scandal sheets and way over Winger's inexperienced head. The prosecution has the murder weapon, the motive, and the eyewitness who puts the defendant at the scene. It's apparent from the reaction to the prosecution's opening statement that the jury and the press have already found Redford's new client guilty as charged.

This is an open-and-shut case. Picture a packed courtroom and a circus-like atmosphere as the district attorney finishes his powerful introduction. How should Redford proceed? How could he possibly shift the pendulum even a little away from the powerfully negative and toward the neutral? He begins his opening remarks in a normal fashion. "Ladies and gentlemen, Chelsea Deardon did not kill Victor Taft. The prosecution has suggested a possible motive, but one based entirely on hearsay, conjecture, and circumstantial evidence, evidence that on the surface would appear to have some substance, but upon closer examination will prove to have no relevance whatsoever to this case." Okay, a decent start, but the camera tells us that Redford's remarks are falling on deaf ears in the jury box. He sees this as well. Redford stops suddenly, looks into the eyes of the jurors, tilts his head in that winning way of his and says, "You're not buying this, are you? You're not listening to a word I'm saying. Really. Right?" He pauses. Then, "Guess what? I don't blame you. After listening to the prosecution's evidence, even *I'm* convinced my client murdered Victor Taft. After all, if I'd walked into the room and found Victor Taft dead on the floor and Chelsea Deardon's fingerprints all over the weapon that killed him, there isn't much in the world that wouldn't convince me she was guilty. Look, let's just save ourselves a lot of time here. Who thinks Chelsea Deardon is guilty?" When Redford asks for a show of hands on this question, the prosecution objects. The judge grumbles.

Redford continues, "Come on. I've got my hand raised. I believe that my client murdered Victor Taft in cold blood. Who agrees with me? Come on!" More objections, more grumbles. "Let's save the State of New York a lot of time and money and move directly to sentencing." Redford has gone so negative even his co-counsel, who didn't know what was coming, is having her doubts. The defendant is beside herself. With the courtroom now in chaos, the judge calling for order, and reporters racing for the phones, Redford places himself near the jury box, where one respectable-looking middle-aged woman (played by the actress who later in her career played Jerry Seinfeld's mother) asks softly, "Isn't she entitled to a fair trial?" Redford replies instantly, "Oh, let's give her a fair trial and *then* convict her."

By now the judge has had enough. He disqualifies the jury and threatens Redford with contempt. Redford begs the judge's indulgence. He says he's perfectly happy with this jury and has faith in them, even though they believe his client is guilty. The prosecutor expresses his satisfaction with this jury, and the judge relents.

Brilliant negotiating by Redford. With the emotional pendulum set solidly in the negative area in the beginning, he *agreed* with the jury's negative perspective. What was he trying to accomplish? Waking up the jury to their bias and planting a second thought. By joining their decision of "no," he was enticing them to remember their oath as jurors, enticing them into a slightly more moderate opposition. He also had their full attention now. The jurors were still negative, but at least they were thinking. Then he said, "You're not listening to a word I'm saying." Another negative strip line. Then, "Guess what. I don't blame you." Another one!

How many negative strip lines are required in a given negotiation is always a judgment call, but a good rule of thumb is to continue until you see, or sense, evidence of significant movement by that pendulum from the harshly negative zone. When Redford finally feels the movement with this jury, he subtly introduces the presumption of innocence: "So we all think she's guilty. Now what do we do? It's a dilemma, isn't it? It's an especially difficult problem, because we've developed a legal concept in this country to protect ourselves, to protect our rights. It's called the presumption of innocence."

And you can guess that Darryl Hannah is soon found innocent, or, rather, the case against her is dismissed when the actual murderer is discovered. *Legal Eagles* is definitely not a great movie, but that was a great set of negative strip lines by Robert Redford. Hats off.

Returning to the real world, recall the earlier story from Chapter 3 about Mike, the senior VP at Zete who got tangled up in the bogus claim for damages from the Fortune 100 corporation. Mike wasn't afraid to say no to the Fortune 100 team, because this was a straightforward warranty issue. Now I want to add a few more details. In the course of the protracted negotiation, Larry, whom Mike had appointed as Zete's new lead negotiator, called Charles, head legal counsel for the Fortune 100 company. Charles immediately and brusquely informed Larry that he saw no chance of avoiding a lawsuit. Furthermore, his procurement and business units were so fed up with Zete that news of this debacle had made it all the way to the corner office, top floor.

Larry wasn't taken aback. Far from it. He immediately *agreed* with Charles—a negative strip line—and then added, "It's probably even worse than that, Charles. I don't see how we can ever recover. Even if we went to court and were found to be contractually correct, I don't see how we'll ever be an acceptable supplier for you again."

Silence—a long silence. The only thing Charles had not expected following his indictment was *a seemingly more negative position* from the other party. Finally he said that Larry could be correct. Larry again acknowledged all of Zete's failures and the general impossibility of the situation. What a snafu. This was another negative strip line, followed by another long pause. Then Charles asked Larry how long he had been on the account. Larry said he had just come aboard and was struggling to find a leg for Zete to stand on. *Another* negative strip line, greeted again by a long pause. Then Charles suggested that he and Larry get together before anyone did anything rash, and they should bring Mike into the loop as well. Now it was Larry's turn to be surprised. Of course he knew the value of the negative strip line, but Larry's reopening of the negotiation, in effect, after the door had been slammed shut was all Larry could ask for. Larry admitted he was a bit surprised and very pleased with the invitation to a meeting with Charles and Mike. Fairly soon, as I've already reported, the warranty hassle was resolved and the two companies signed agreements worth a cool $180 million.

Several years ago, the Dixie Chicks, the highest-selling female group in any music genre, got into trouble because of remarks made by lead singer Natalie Maines about President Bush at a performance in London. In their movie *Shut Up and Sing,* which chronicles the highs, lows, and mayhem that ensued, Ms. Maines, at another performance, reiterates her belief in the freedom of speech and invites the audience to express their feelings about the Dixie Chicks: *Go ahead, boo us if you want to.* A negative strip line for sure from downstage, front and center. What happened? The crowd went wild. Now, maybe only the fans sympathetic to their political position attended the concert. Maybe they'd lost their other fans for good. Regardless, the negative strip line was a good negotiating move. Like the positive strip line, it never fails to lower the pressure, lessen any neediness on your part, and give you a bit of a fresh start.

Test Drive Find a good opportunity without much at stake and say, "Wow, this is bad. I don't know if we'll ever recover. What a mess." It is quite likely that the other side will then *help* you recover. It's so much fun when this happens.

THE PRESENTATION

If you work on building vision and painting problems with effective questions, you have already made a winning presentation. In opening my defense of this position against the formal presentation, I pose these interrogative-led questions: When was the last time you hoped that the salesperson/agent/ whomever would just be quiet for five minutes and let you discover the offer for yourself? How many times have you walked into an upscale store and a salesperson immediately attached himself to you like a limpet? Plenty, I imagine. Most of us would rather be left alone to look around for ourselves, and then to find help and ask questions when we're ready.

**The greatest presentation you will ever give is
the one the other party never sees.**

Justin is a great case in point. He was fairly successful in commercial real estate and was initially as skeptical of my system as anyone who has ever worked with me. The first words to me as we discussed the basics of the system were "This business about 'no presentation' won't work. You have to present something first to get their attention. You have to take charge and let them see what you are bringing to the table." This principle and others seemed so contrarian as to be somehow "countercultural," and Justin is not a counterculture kind of guy. I'm surprised he stayed on board with us. But he did, and he eventually became sold on the system, thanks to an episode involving a presentation in a deal he had lost.

In Justin's mind, the "no" received after his presentation meant that the negotiation was over. Time to move on. I saw an opportunity to practice and learn. I coached Justin and he executed our plan flawlessly, beginning with his admission that his presentation had missed the mark. Where, exactly, had he fallen short? Impressed by Justin's frank admission, probably influenced by Justin's un-okayness, the buyer who had previously spurned him opened up and admitted that he still hadn't found the right property. He asked Justin if he had another presentation he'd like to give. And Justin did a great thing. He said, "No, I don't. What I think will help us the most is the clearest possible picture of what you're looking for." Justin then asked many questions and came away with the picture he should have had months before. The other man had had his vision all along. Justin just hadn't discovered it. Now that he had, he went to work and found the perfect property, and the rest is history. Although Justin will now "present" under the right circumstances, he's certainly not beholden to the practice. Justin is a good negotiator, but he is not a magician—and he doesn't need to be. Whether he's dealing with a city zoning board or a Japanese conglomerate, he concentrates on research and building vision. He has learned that the main problem with the formal presentation is that it puts the other side into the overtly intellectual and judgmental mode. When people get into this mode, what happens? They raise objections. Think about this from your own experience. When someone "presents" to you, formally or informally, your instinct is to hunt for objections, quibbles, and mistakes, and you often find them. The classic presentation serves only to create objections, so the presenter ends up *answering* questions rather than *asking* them.

If you have worked effectively to build vision, if you have effectively painted the picture of the problems for the other side, a presentation is simply a waste of time and energy. If you have *not* painted that picture and built that vision, the presentation is no substitute for your failure to do so, and it won't do you any good now. What are you going to present? How do you know that the points of your presentation have any interest? You don't, because you don't have a clear vision of their issues and problems. So people who want to "present" to me are telling me that they don't really understand my problems. If they did understand them, they wouldn't be presenting blindly, throwing mud at the wall and hoping that some of it sticks.

Furthermore, a presentation shows neediness, doesn't it? Can't it often seem like a rush to close? Can't it come across as taking away the right to say no? Indeed it can and does.

Perhaps you want to present because this negotiation is going nowhere, and the presentation is your last hope.

Or maybe the other party, a shrewd team, has insisted on the formal presentation as a ploy. So you do your thing and lay it all out and show 'em how great you are. This accomplishes what, really? Don't take my word for it. Think honestly about your own experience and I'll bet you agree that otherwise effective negotiations have *survived* formal presentations, but they have never needed them.

I need a presentation on your business.

What area would you like me to focus on? (You have spoken slowly and calmly, of course, nodding your head.)

Well, we've been buying all our widgets from U.S. Widgets and we'd like to compare your capabilities with theirs.

Great. What area should we focus on first? (Slowly and calmly, and nodding.)

I think we should start with facilities.

I can certainly do that. Our manufacturing is centrally located in the major population centers. What's most important to you about our facilities?

Well, we have to be sure about capacity. We have some major expansion in our strategic plan, and we think we're going to require a considerable capacity capability with two suppliers.

What levels of capacity are you targeting?

At peak it will require one million units per week. Can you do that?

Good question. Just ballpark, when does the plan call for peak?

About eighteen months out. Can you do that?

That's a good question. I'll have to do some research on that. I should start with your engineers. When could I meet with them to understand the specs and requirements?

I'll arrange for a meeting sometime in the next two weeks.

That's not an entirely fanciful exchange. It's an effective way to deal with a request for a presentation and an effective way to get the ball rolling. If you had jumped right in with a presentation, you would have been guessing about what the buyer actually wanted and needed (from your perspective) to see. Instead, use your principles, ask questions, get into their world, know their real problems (capacity seems to be one here), and build vision. Do all this and if you do end up making the formal presentation, at least you'll be able to do it well.

There is no good reason to "present" until you know exactly what the presentation should look like. That's rule number one on this subject. Furthermore, be certain that you are presenting to the real decision-makers. If you make a formal presentation to the "unqualified," to people who can't really make decisions, you're really wasting your time. Be sure to have an agenda negotiated in advance of the big day. (Agendas are the subject of an upcoming chapter.) The other people must know, *Okay, here we go, the formal presentation.* They must know what the presentation will contain, and what it will not contain. They must know that it is finally yes-or-no time. "Maybe" is not allowed as an answer following the presentation. Make sure this agreement is negotiated on an agenda. If it's not, what will you do when you hear the dreaded "maybe"? Finally—and I hope by this point this statement almost goes without saying—always present in *their world.* Granted, you're telling them things rather than letting them see, but at least tell them things about the issues that are driving the negotiation. Present *only* the information that addresses their issues, problems, and concerns—or what you know about them, which may not be much or you wouldn't be presenting in the first place.

Resist the temptation to throw in the kitchen sink. If the only problem is the tire's maximum carrying capacity, forget about how extra-wide your tires are. You can always bring it up later, if the occasion arises. ("Addition by subtraction": This old sports adage about making your team better by getting rid of a certain player is also true for presentations.) Present in the order of importance, as you think you see it. *Mr. Smith, since your most important concern is horsepower, let's look at the engine first. Then we'll check out the headroom for the driver's seat, since you're rather tall and maybe that's also important to you.*

A high school football player who was being recruited used my ideas in his search for a college. He never made a formal application to the school he finally chose—and that chose him. He did provide a demonstration—a videotape—and the key point about his demonstration pertains to presentations. Most recruits make the mistake of submitting film that is in their own world: clips of their spectacular runs, spectacular catches, TDs. But is this what the coach really wants to see? If it's not, if the coach's real concern is otherwise, the recruit has not presented to that concern. The way to find out is to ask the question this recruit asked of every coach: *"How do you evaluate a player?"* Isn't this question just common sense? Yes. But is it commonly asked? No. Our recruit found out that the answer varied from coach to coach and often seemed very limited. One coach was mainly interested in vertical jumping ability, another in speed, and another in strength work (specifically, the bench press). One coach would not recruit a defensive back under six feet tall, and another would not recruit any players under six feet tall. No coach said or implied, *Send me clips of your greatest plays.* So our recruit tailored his videotape to the answers provided by each coach. He "presented" in the world of each specific coach, not his own world. He showed them what he had learned that *they* wanted to see, not what he thought they should want to see, or what he wanted to see of himself. That approach took a lot of discipline and a lot of work.

In short, if you insist on making a formal presentation, or if a hidebound (or stealthy) negotiator insists that you make one, at least do it well. Use your principles. It's perfectly okay to pull out all the stops with overheads, art, graphics, multimedia, and everything else that PowerPoint and the other software programs offer, but none of this works if you're relying on the glitz by itself to carry the day. It won't. If your high-tech presentation doesn't address the vision and the problems of the other side, you're wasting your gigabytes. (And if you've negotiated well up to this point, you will find that they won't see your presentation.)

Three-Minute Checklist

- You cannot tie down a significant point too many times. Three times is the minimum, three-plus even better.
- The pendulum needs to be near the middle—not too positive, not too negative. This is where the good agreements are found.
- When the excitement builds, consider tapping the brake with a positive strip line. It can only help.
- When a negative mood sets in, consider acknowledging the fact with a negative strip line. *Join* the negativity and thereby invite the other party to join you, step back, and take a second look.
- If you have discovered problems and built vision, the formal presentation shouldn't be necessary. If you do have to present, be sure the presentation addresses their problems and builds their vision.

8

The Truth Is, You Don't Know

Blank-Slating to Success

All the possible traps you can fall into in a negotiation—
the fear of saying and hearing no, failure to build vision
on the other side, too much talking, not enough listening
to answers and thoughts even after asking good questions—
are all often rooted in yet another one: unwarranted assumptions and expectations.

You may fear saying no because you assume the other side
will be offended or expects to hear yes or maybe. But do you
have any real idea where they stand, what they're after, or what
they expect? Not at first, you don't. You may feel neediness to
sign this agreement because you assume the other side, notori-
ous for its ruthlessness, has no neediness of its own. But you
don't know this. You must find out. You may fail to build vision
on the other side because you assume it's already clear. *Who
could miss this?* They could.

Most of the readers of this book have been trained to take
pride in their consummate knowledge, but any such tendency
to "know" interferes with blank-slating. If you know, why
bother to ask questions and listen closely to the answers? If the

choice is between knowing everything and knowing nothing, you're much better off in a negotiation knowing nothing, starting from scratch, asking questions, and finding out about their world. Likewise, it's so easy to fall into the "they're going to think . . . they're going to think . . . they're going to think" trap and forget you have no idea what they're *actually* thinking.

Assumptions and expectations are everywhere in negotiation—around every corner, behind every door. They're a major problem, but the good news is that with discipline you can guard against them by creating a *blank slate* in your own mind, which then sits ready and waiting to receive any new information, new attitudes, new emotions, new *anything* that the other folks wittingly or unwittingly beam your way. It is through blank-slating that you learn what's really going on in a negotiation, what's really holding things up, what the real issues are, and what the real vision is. With blank-slating, you will never again get deep into a negotiation before you realize: *Wait a minute, she agrees that we need a new marketing plan! I wish I'd known that. I never just asked her. All this time I'd assumed . . .*

> **Be a blank slate. Work with the best**
> **possible facts and information,**
> **not with assumptions and expectations**
> **that are so often dead wrong.**

Boy, are we glad to see you, Todd. Can you deliver five thousand widgets next month? You can, and you'll be happy to, because it would be an unprecedented order from this small outfit, but right now you do *not* answer yes. That would be making all kinds of unwarranted assumptions and entail all sorts of unwarranted expectations, wouldn't it? Here are the obvious ones: You're assuming the company has the cash to pay for 5,000 widgets, because you run a cash business, but maybe they'll want terms for this large order. You're not expecting a request for a price concession, but such a request could be a plausible next step for them to take, couldn't it? You're assuming that the order can't be *10,000* widgets. Such a number really would be unbelievable, but maybe this company is now operating in a whole new world that you don't know about. You're assuming the "next month" stipulation isn't important, even though you've never heard it from this account. All in all, why would you expect the background for this unprecedented order of 5,000 to be exactly the same as it has been for the regular order of 2,000? In fact, something *must* be going on. For the sake of this order, perhaps, and for the future, definitely, it behooves you to try to find out what it is.

So what do you do? You blank-slate, obey your rule of 3+, and ask good interrogative-led questions, preceded by a tiny bit of nurturing. *Five thousand? Jane, that's a big order. What's changed?* You listen to the answer. You ask another good question. Why 5,000? You listen carefully to the answer. You ask another question. When must they be delivered by? Again, you listen carefully as you complete your rule of 3+. Maybe you find out something interesting in the end, or maybe Jane is hush-hush and really does just want the widgets and has the cashier's check ready to go, full price for 5,000 widgets. Either way, you move your mission and purpose forward. You have controlled any possible neediness and stayed within your system. You were ready for any possible second surprise Jane might have sprung on you, and you were ready to capitalize on anything you did learn. That's smart negotiating. Immediately jumping up and yelling yes is something less (amateur hour, frankly).

Remember the new swimming pool you're buying? Pete the contractor acknowledges that there have been some problems, but now—late April—he announces that the Memorial Day completion is a lock, no problem. Now, think about this. As the somewhat anxious homeowner, what would be your *instinctive* response, given the preceding problems? That's right. You'd ask some questions. *That sounds great, Pete, but what about the tile shipment? When will it arrive? What word do you have from the supplier? What have they said? How long will that part of the job take?*

This is the mindset, the blank-slate mindset, you want to have in every phase of every negotiation.

**Always blank-slate.
It's *impossible* to overdo it.**

Once you get the hang of it, you become so focused and locked onto the moment that you almost feel you're stepping out of your body, going to a corner of the room, and watching yourself negotiate. It's an exhilarating feeling. I've seen many individuals reap immense satisfaction from a really good episode of blank-slating, that moment when they realized that a tiny little unexamined assumption on their part had been the main problem in the entire negotiation.

YOUR POSITIVE EXPECTATIONS ARE KILLERS

How many times have you heard one of these statements from the other side in a negotiation?

"It looks terrific."

"Nothing stands in the way now."

"No question this is the best that's available on the market today."

"Let's meet and put this thing to bed."

"Man, you're just the person we've been waiting for!"

"Well, my numbers do have some flexibility."

"I can't believe how on-target you all are."

"This is a perfect fit. We can go the distance with it."

With all such remarks—and they are infinite in their variety—what's really going on? Quite often, that negotiator is building your positive expectations to close the deal. If you buy into these statements, you'll be taken advantage of for sure.

It looks perfect, Sam. Hearing this remark, do you think, "She's actually buying this; I have a live one here"? If so, you're looking for trouble. You're getting excited, you're getting needy, and you're already stepping smack into all manner of unwarranted assumptions and expectations. Your guard is down, and sure enough, here it comes: The buyer cuts your legs out from under you. *How big a discount can you give us?* Now what? Your emotional pendulum has just swung from the too strongly positive to the too strongly negative. You bought into the positive expectation of the big sale, and now you gulp and buy into the negative expectation of a big discount. *It's normally four hundred dollars per unit, Tammy, but if you buy ten, I can give you fifteen percent.* Let the compromising games begin. *That's not enough, Sam. Surely you can do better than that.*

Now you're really in trouble, all because you got caught up in those positive expectations triggered by *It looks perfect.* If you had blank-slated instead, if you had taken that teaser for what it was worth—nothing, really—you wouldn't have given the buyer a discount figure. You would have nurtured and asked a question to create a clear vision: *Good question, Tammy. I don't have the authority to negotiate a discount, but what quantity are you thinking about?*

These "positive expectations" games are practically SOP in the corporate world, often in the context of a request for your "best price." Say that everyone at the table knows that the going price for the widget is $1,000 per unit. This possible new customer announces that of course they have other suppliers, but now they really want to consolidate all of their widget purchases—1,000 units—with one supplier in order to get the best price. What happens when you get the scent of such an order? If you're not careful, if you don't blank-slate, an equation starts dancing in your brain: 1,000 x $1,000 = *$1,000,000.* Even with a volume discount thrown in, this counts as real money for your business. This deal would be a triumph for you. And that dynamic of prematurely raised expectations is *exactly* what the other side was counting on.

Suckered in by your own excitement and neediness, you immediately give them the best discounted price for the 1,000 units, expecting them to jump on this number, sign the contract, and open the champagne. But say they don't jump—and they won't, because the champagne can wait and they've played this game many times before with other suppliers, and it almost always works. Instead, they come back and announce that they've decided to spread the purchase of these units among several vendors after all. So they don't need 1,000 from you. Just a couple of hundred, but they want those couple of hundred at the same incredibly good unit price you agreed to for an order five times as large! And by the way, they hint broadly, they're going to be very disappointed if that discount doesn't stick. They'll be very disappointed to hear no.

Now what do you do? Now what are your emotions? Now what good did all those positive expectations do you? If there is one classic maneuver played by many companies and shrewd negotiators in many businesses, this is it: Build positive expectations with pie-in-the-sky numbers, then start in with the ifs, ands, and buts. This gambit is extraordinarily effective when the customer is a big company and the supplier a smaller one. Take Xem, an auto industry supplier with 2,500 employees—a relatively small company for that industry. One of the big auto manufacturers requested that Xem compete for a contract calling for 7 million units, which would be a very large order for Xem. Too large, in fact. Recall Boeing's recent "no" to Southwest Airlines. Same thing here with Xem, a company with a valid mission and purpose that emphasizes quality and dependability and faithfully fulfilling its contracts, and it wasn't going to fall for the "positive expectations" trick. Its team blank-slated, stayed within its mission and purpose and its negotiating principles, took a careful look at its production capability, and said, "No, thanks. We appreciate the invitation, but we can't bid on the seven million. We'd love to bid on three and a half million."

The carmaker was completely flabbergasted, of course. I'll bet that *every* other supplier it had ever dealt with was prostrate on the ground in its efforts to satisfy the corporate giant with the huge order. The carmaker had played these hapless suppliers against one another for decades, and no one at Xem was surprised (for one thing, they are good blank-slaters; for another, they know the car manufacturers) when the carmaker said that Xem would be removed from the list of interested suppliers if it didn't make a proposal for the whole order. Xem repeated that it would love to participate in the opportunity for the 3.5 million units but could not bid for whole order because it didn't have the resources. Please take us off you list for this contract. Two weeks passed before the next communication from the carmaker. *Okay, you may submit a proposal for half of the order.* Submit it Xem did, and they got the order at the price they wanted.

Forget the positive expectations. Stay with your mission and purpose and your principles. But it's easier said than done, I realize. Positive expectations are so *positive.* They feel so good. Who doesn't want to be hopeful? After all, Woody Hayes, the legendary coach of Ohio State football, said, "The most important thing is not winning, it is having the hope to win. As long as you have hope you have life." Anyone who has played competitive sports has probably been coached about the virtues of a "positive attitude." This sounds great, and often it is great, but for a negotiator a positive attitude is just another, more seductive way of saying positive *expectations.* So for the negotiator, even a positive attitude is dangerous. Yes, it's true. That attitude can evolve into expectations that can and probably will evolve into neediness. After all, it is emotional!

When I say blank-slate, I mean *blank*-slate. And this takes incredible discipline, which doesn't come overnight, but it does come with effort and practice.

Test Drive When things seem to be going your way in some little negotiation around the office or the home, when you sense the triumph of victory, and when your positive expectations are really kicking in—*don't* act on them. Call a time-out, suggest a break for coffee or for lunch, and take the opportunity to blank-slate, to see clearly. It can't hurt you. It can only help you.

YOUR NEGATIVE EXPECTATIONS
ARE ALSO KILLERS

In negotiations, the other side may try to draw you into positive expectations or they may try *negative* expectations before things even get started. Consider the widget priced at $1,000 from the scenario mentioned earlier. Instead of tossing out the bait of a possible order for 1,000 units, then trying to lower that order drastically while still demanding the deeply discounted price, this time the customer announces up front that they know the deeply discounted price and want that price for this small order. They stipulate this at the beginning of negotiations. Now you may not have positive expectations but negative ones: either no deal at all or a deal so heavily discounted that it might as well be no deal at all.

Ignore such negative thoughts. Recognize that the early numbers are just that and nothing more: early numbers of no real significance. Rest confident in your knowledge that there's nothing in your mission and purpose about busting the rate sheet just because this customer wants you to. Simply say, "Gee, we're sorry. We just can't sell a couple of hundred widgets to anyone, even you folks, with whom we'd love to do business, for the deep discount. Maybe you could try to buy them from U.S. Widget at that price."

And maybe they will. In any event, you haven't busted your rate sheet right off the bat; you haven't set an early compromise precedent. You have blank-slated and nurtured, and you wait for the reply. Now let's turn this negotiation around. You're the customer looking for a new widget supplier, and if you're not careful you, too, will also be susceptible to positive and negative expectations—positive when the supplier says, *Sure, we can gear up to provide a thousand widgets by next month. . . . Absolutely. . . . I guarantee it,* or negative when the supplier says, *Oh, I don't think we could ever meet that delivery date. Sorry.* Take all such remarks as initial decisions (or tactics) to be followed by other decisions (and tactics).

Perhaps the most pervasive, straightforward example of negative expectations is when you're dealing with someone, or with an entire company, that has always been difficult to work with, maybe even been more trouble than they were worth. This is what you feel after every negotiation with these troublesome people. Well, maybe they *are* more trouble than they're worth, and if they are you make that decision and cut your losses. But you do so calmly and rationally, not because they're a pain in the you-know-where. Tomorrow they may *not* be a pain in the you-know-where, for whatever reason, or maybe they do remain a pain in the you-know-where, but so what? The question is whether you can negotiate with this company.

Quite a few years ago I had a client, Gene, who was a sales rep in San Francisco. He paid one particular customer a regular visit on the first Friday morning of every month. He did this for almost a year without receiving an order. Now, here was a sales rep with every reason to develop negative expectations, and the failure to make a sale was certainly frustrating, but keeping in touch was no trouble (the would-be customer's address was very convenient to the rep's usual route around the Bay Area), my client really liked this individual personally, and he didn't succumb to negative expectations. One day Gene missed his morning call but knocked on the door late that afternoon. And here was what might as well have been a different guy! He gave Gene an order that very day! Of course Gene blank-slated some more and asked, among other questions, "Why the order now, after a year?" The man replied, "Well, I'm diabetic and it takes me a couple hours in the morning to get my blood sugar under control. I have trouble getting started until about ten. Come to think of it, I don't think I ever place an order until the afternoon, probably out of habit. I appreciate your continuing to come to see me."

Ouch! My client's grade on this exam could certainly be marked down for failing to create vision for his customer—but not for negative expectations and not for a failure to blank-slate.

Neither positive nor negative expectations have any place in your work. You blank-slate and you *negotiate*, that's all.

Perhaps the worst danger of all for men and women in straight sales is the generalized negative expectation that can set in following a series of lost deals. What happens to the emotional state of individuals stuck in these ruts? If they're not very careful, such negative expectations can have a terribly debilitating effect. The dreaded S-word—"slump"—comes to mind. Surely negative expectations play some role when an athlete goes into a slump, and negotiators, too, certainly those in direct sales, do have slumps. Banish slumps by banishing expectations.

Test Drive Select a day on which you will keep the most complete list possible of the expectations, both positive and negative, great and small, that you feel creeping into your thinking and attitude. You walk into a meeting and everyone's laughing beforehand? It's probably time to note your positive expectation. Or everyone is sulking? It'll be hard to resist negative expectation! Write it down. Of course, we all know the first meeting could easily be a loser and the second a great success.

THE TRUTH IS, YOU DON'T KNOW

Now, what about assumptions, the other chief obstacle to effective blank-slating? They're just as dangerous as expectations, and just as common, maybe even more common. Most of us eventually come to believe that we're pretty good at "reading" other people, at understanding what they're really feeling and thinking. Negotiators, in particular, tend to pride themselves on their "people skills." Experts in every field pride themselves in their grasp of all subjects relating to their expertise.

The human event with the most tragic consequences is warfare. Set aside the question of the wisdom and justice of all the wars down the ages. How many lives in those hundreds of wars have been lost and wasted because of unwarranted assumptions on the part of those making the so-called strategic decisions? Of course, World War I is exhibit number one, a colossal tragedy rooted in woefully blind and therefore stupid miscalculations. In Vietnam, successive administrations were absolutely certain they knew what the North Vietnamese were thinking and how they would react to bombing halts, bombing resumptions, peace feelers, and all of our other futile attempts to obtain "peace with honor." Absolutely certain and absolutely wrong. Over three decades later, we know this. And how about the assumption that the end of "official" hostilities between the uniformed armies in the spring of 2003 would be the end of the matter in Iraq, Mission Accomplished?

Back to business. Time and again I will ask a room full of individual and corporate negotiation students how they prepare for a negotiation. They say:

I want to get to know how the other side thinks.

I want to get into their heads.

I want to understand them. If I can do that, then I can figure out what they're going to do.

Sounds okay. Sounds like their world. But wait. These students will then turn right around and say:

I know what they'll do if we make that offer.

I know how they think.

They won't budge without a volume discount.

They won't do that. I know what they'll do.

I know them and they will drop the whole program.

The theoretical intention to blank-slate is quickly set aside in favor of making assumptions. It's almost human nature, I've decided. There are a million assumptions lying in wait to ambush you and a million ways to fall into the trap. My client Oscar submitted a proposal for a $25 million acquisition. Because he was so confident he knew the whole story behind this deal—because he assumed he knew the whole story—he didn't ask for a six-month exclusive. Oscar *knew* they wouldn't give him one. And Oscar didn't ask for a confidentiality document, because he *knew* they wouldn't give him one, or even for a nondisclosure agreement. What happened next was simple and predictable. The other side immediately hired an investment banker, who shopped Oscar's proposal with three other potential buyers. Oscar then found himself in an auction that drove the price up to $60 million. He won the auction, but at what unnecessary cost? I can only conjecture how much less he might have paid if he hadn't gotten into the bidding war he brought upon himself because of his grand (and expensive) assumption.

It's no surprise that assumptions are often based on what you think you know. It may be surprising that assumptions can also be based on your *success*. That's right. You try a trick or tactic in one negotiation, it works, and you think you know why it worked. In the next negotiation, you give yourself permission not to blank-slate or dig in with the questions—with the vision. Instead, you do exactly what worked the last time. After all, you're smart and successful and you get paid to know this stuff. The more success you have, the more convinced you are that you know all you need to know. Assumption follows assumption. A vicious cycle indeed. And plenty of people get away with this, let's face it. In effect, they're pursuing and achieving a performance goal—a modest performance goal. They've made some deals, and that's good enough. It's not my role to criticize such a decision. Some people would rather play golf four or five times a week, and that's their call. It is my role to point out that if you, on the other hand, want to be the best and most successful negotiator you can be, letting some degree of success lull you into assumptions and expectations *will* cost you in the long run. Recall the scenario with Jane asking Todd if he can deliver an unprecedented 5,000 widgets next month. Sure Todd could have whipped out the paperwork and *perhaps* have signed the deal. Let's say he did. If so, what did he learn about the new set of facts that must have lurked behind that order? Nothing. His easy success came at a price. A good negotiator does not want to pay that price, and doesn't have to.

How many times have you gone into a meeting for one reason, only to find out that you were there for a completely different reason? Phil had traveled to Washington, D.C., to meet with a client team to discuss changes in the contract they were working on. He had prepared diligently for the meeting and was ready to offer some great new ideas. When he got to the meeting, however, the team threw him a complete curveball. They wanted the contract to stand as is. What! Totally flustered, Phil dropped his blank slate and allowed the assumptions to come pouring into his fertile imagination. *Uh-oh, something has happened. Conditions have changed. Are they suddenly unhappy with me? My work is down the drain.* Actually, what the client really wanted was Phil's input on a completely new and different project. That's what they wanted to talk about, not the old contract. That was ancient history—for the time being. They even asked for Phil's "best guess" on the cost of the new direction.

Now, Phil is an excellent negotiator, proving that just about anyone can lose focus and fall into the assumptions trap. I asked him what happened next. *Well, I wasn't prepared, and I told them so in as nice a way as possible. I explained I was caught completely off-guard and that I'd have to get back to them.* This wasn't a disaster. Phil kept his decision process going, and he "lived to perform another day."

Most experienced businesspeople can recall when they didn't even bother calling on a potential client or supplier or customer because they assumed this deal would never work out, only to learn later that it might well have worked out. Many industries are tightly knit communities, a seamless web within which executives and sales reps move easily from company to company. In the semiconductor world, it's not uncommon to sell to Bill at Intel this year and two years later run into him functioning in the same capacity at Applied. Maybe you had a tough time delivering for Bill when he was at Intel. If so, you may have to fight the assumption that he remembers that problem (in this assumption, you're probably right) *and* that he'll hold it against you in his new job at Applied (in this assumption you could be totally wrong, so don't make it).

Barbara used to work for Jonathan at Humongous, didn't she? They're terrible. Maybe Humongous is terrible, but what does that tell you about Barbara? Nothing. *Maybe Barbara has changed.* Forget whether she's "changed." Start all over with her. Blank slate. *It took Humongous three years to get that done the last time.* What does last time have to do with this time? Maybe a lot, maybe nothing. The only way to find out is to blank-slate.

Make absolutely no mistake about it: Hidden assumptions are everywhere, and they're just as dangerous for you in negotiation as unwarranted expectations, because they're so subtle and insidious.

Vague statements draw us into making a lot of our assumptions.

"When can this be done?"

"Pretty soon."

Well, what does "pretty soon" mean? This morning, this afternoon, tomorrow, next week, next month? Always be on the lookout for such soft, ambiguous answers. Make no assumptions. Keep asking your good questions. Pin it down. Or say your acquaintance Annemarie, top assistant to the CEO at a company with which you do a lot of business, tells you in passing that she's retiring—at age fifty-four. If your blank slate is in good operating condition, you don't say, *Hey, great, Annemarie. I wish you the best of luck.* You say, *Hey, great, Annemarie. I wish you the best of luck. But I'm surprised. You've always seemed so happy at Humongous. Why are you leaving?* Now you may find out something you need to know, something about changes at Humongous, something about the future of the CEO. I admit that this is one of my stagier, more far-fetched scenarios, but I'm sticking with it to emphasize how complete and thorough your blank slate should be. Annemarie's retirement from Humongous at age fifty-four really should lead to some questions on your part.

Take the word "expensive." It means very different things to a CEO and to a schoolteacher, and—here's the important kicker—the CEO probably assumes that anyone using the term means what the CEO has in mind, and likewise with the teacher. In the case of the CEO, this can be a major mistake. Here's an excellent case study on that point.

Bob, my client for more than fifteen years, was meeting with the CEO of an up-and-coming equipment company for purposes of finalizing the price the CEO would be able to pay for new technology Bob's company had developed. As Bob tells the story,

We had been discussing the opportunity afforded his company by the technology, the opportunity it presented in terms of market share, and of course the impact the acquisition of the technology would have on Wall Street's perception of his company. I had built his vision, goodness knows. I was confident of that. When he finally asked about price, I said, "It will be expensive, for obvious reasons." He asked me to be specific. "Well," I said, "we haven't set a price. We plan to sell it to the highest bidder." I asked him if he had a number he would put on the technology. He asked me about my authority. If he gave a number that was satisfactory to me, did I have the authority to make the agreement. "Yes," I replied. "I have full board authority." I said that if he wanted to give me a number, I'd be happy to decline it or accept it then and there. I was shocked by his high number. He had set the bar very high. I told him that I appreciated his offer but nevertheless rejected it with the expressed hope that he would think through his offer, think about this technology, and reconsider. I asked him if we could come together by the end of the week for a last and final discussion. He agreed and in that meeting raised his number. He paid us seventy-five percent more than we would have asked for and accepted.

Expensive? The CEO heard that word and plugged in his own number.

Test Drive Select a day in which you're going to make a conscious effort to identify every assumption you make and every assumption you see and hear others make. By definition, almost every use of the phrase "I think" will be followed by an assumption. Keep a running list. Be ready with more sheets of paper. Every surprise, no matter how small (the unfriendly guy behind the coffee counter, say), is probably the result of an assumption (that service people will be friendly, for example). Be sure to include the driver who goes on green without looking left and right. At the end of the day you'll be stunned by the assumptions made and observed. Most will be harmless enough. Some might not be. In negotiation, most will definitely not be harmless.

Here's some good news. You can also *plant* assumptions — and if the opposing parties let you, why not? That's what Bob was doing with his use of the word "expensive" in the negotiation with the CEO. As it happens, I have a neighbor, Dick, who has practically made a living by planting assumptions in a non-threatening way and then reaping the benefit as those assumptions drive the other side's decisions. (By the way, he adopted this negotiating stance long before we had any discussions about my blank-slate principle.) Example: Dick recently went into the hardware and garden supply store to purchase a new lawn mower. He'd had his eye on one for several months. The salesman approached.

May I help you?

I have my eye on this riding lawn mower.

Oh, that's a dandy.

It sure is.

Now what do you think the salesman might have a positive expectation about right now? You think he might be making some unwarranted assumptions? You can bet on it, I'm afraid, and Dick was ready to spring his trap. He looked straight at the salesman.

Why that price?

Sir?

Why that price?

[pause] Wait right here! Let me see what I can do.

Five minutes later Dick reaped a 30 percent discount. The salesman assumed that's what Dick was driving for, and he assumed that Dick wouldn't have bought the machine without the discount. But he didn't know this.

E-mails are a particularly easy place to plant assumptions, because we read and reply to most of them so quickly.

> It is required by our policy that we have a contract in place. My CEO is very interested in your success, but the reality is we have no options without a signed contract.

Where's the planted assumption? If you didn't catch it the first time, study the statement again. Hint: It's a single word.

That word is "policy." Everyone has policies. Some are binding and others are not. In this case, the policy isn't, but the writer is hoping that the reader makes the quick assumption that it is.

DO YOUR RESEARCH

You can dispense with many assumptions with a series of clicks with your favorite mouse. In the age of Google and Ask and Yahoo! and all the other search engines, research is easier than it has ever been. Obviously, research is one of your best tools in getting rid of unwarranted assumptions, and there is really no good excuse for not doing the job well. Twenty years ago, the library was a few blocks away. What a chore! Today, the Web is right in front of you. Use it. For my client Tess, whose business deals with intellectual property rights and patents, such research is indispensable. Her company spends thousands of hours annually researching and pursuing violations. One of their more significant discoveries was the nefarious group of companies that had been illegally using patented packaging for more than five years. Long and heated negotiations ensued. At their conclusion, the companies at fault collectively paid royalties of more than $200 million. Other clients have confronted aggressive multinationals that know virtually everything about their suppliers and customers. Regarding the competing suppliers, they know the financial condition of each one, the strengths and weaknesses of each one, their negotiating strategies, their negotiating successes and failures, the decision-making hierarchy, and personal details about the key decision-makers—education, college, awards, family, pets, golf handicap, etc. I am not kidding.

But this is not the norm in American business. A client in Silicon Valley told me not long ago that his small, fairly low-budget negotiating team regularly outresearches the teams from Fortune 100 companies. Smaller companies, partnerships, professionals, and freelancers *usually* come up short in their research. I am amazed by the number of negotiations conducted without even the most basic research: going to the Web, to the business papers and magazines, to the financial statements and year-end reports in order to study the companies, the industry, the marketplace, everything of relevance. That's been my experience, I'm afraid. Please correct me if I'm wrong in your case.

Let's return to that mock negotiation in which the customer, a large corporation, wants the same volume discount for a couple of hundred widgets that your company, a supplier, usually gives for much larger orders. That corporation initially asked about your capacity to deliver 1,000 units, but let's say you've done your research. You therefore know something about the corporation. You've got a good idea of who their competitors are. You know the market for their products. You've read every corporate announcement about new sales and customers. And you therefore know that conditions in their business remain virtually the same as they have been for three years: healthy but not booming; no windfalls on the horizon. Maybe they really do want 1,000 units, but 500 or fewer is the likely number. The nerve on their part! Thanks to research, however, thanks to blank-slating, you were well prepared to handle their scheme to drive up your positive expectations with a big number before hitting you with the demand for the heavy discount for the smaller number. Against many negotiators, this time-tested trick might have worked—would have worked. But because you blank-slated, because you had done your research, you knew better. No positive expectations, no ridiculous discounts offered in the flush of initial excitement. I don't know whether you signed an agreement in the end. I do know you didn't sign a bad agreement.

Earlier I cited the tragic consequences of unwarranted assumptions by leadership in warfare throughout history. Now I refer you to an amazing example of *research* during warfare. Throughout the Vietnam War, the Communist North Vietnamese gathered copious data on the captured American pilots. Agents and spies used library archives to learn the names, addresses, and other important information about the pilots' loved ones. The experts in the prison camps then used this information in their ongoing efforts to break the pilots' collective spirit in the hope of extracting useful information.

IT COULDN'T BE SIMPLER

Research is indispensable, but the best, easiest-to-use, most foolproof tool we have at our disposal in order to blank-slate is the simplest one imaginable:

Take great notes.

By its very nature, if you stop to think about the process, note-taking removes you from your own world and directs you into *their* world, where you want to be. The simple act of picking up the pen or pencil moves you in their direction. Note-taking reinforces listening skills. And if you're listening, you're not talking, which is equally good. No talking! An exaggeration, of course, but I discussed the pitfalls of excessive talking earlier, where the subject was neediness. Talking leads straight to neediness. Moreover, talking while listening is pretty tough to pull off. Choose the listening almost every time. If you can't restrain yourself from excessive talking, you'll never be able to blank-slate. Taking notes helps you break any habit of excessive talking.

In seminars, meetings, and negotiations, I can quickly identify the most successful people around the table. They are the ones listening closely and taking notes, effectively silencing their own thoughts and learning as much as they can about everyone else. They are blank-slating and gathering the pieces of the puzzle. (It's important to note that they are not *solving* the puzzle. That comes later, with analysis, with burning the midnight oil.) You must follow the lead of these highly successful individuals. In order to blank-slate effectively, you must make the little voice in your own head be as silent as possible.

Listen and learn. Listen to every word just as closely as the best trial lawyers listen to every word of testimony, as closely as the best clinicians listen to every word of the patient's "presentation." Sigmund Freud taught his student psychiatrists to first just *listen* with the most open possible mind. The diagnosis could come later. When you're listening, your mind does not wander off. You're not thinking about what you want to say next. You don't interrupt or answer your own questions. As you take notes, you can more easily control your emotions. Your nerves are relaxed and your stomach quiets down, and you comfortably settle into the negotiating session. You don't show excitement or disappointment. You are also allowing everyone else to be more okay, because you're taking notes about what they're saying. (Think about it: When someone takes notes as you're speaking, don't you appreciate this? Of course you do.)

The noise of a contentious negotiation can be overwhelming. I mean "noise" literally, on occasion, and figuratively, often. Embedded in the racket are lots of nonverbal cues and clues, and your good notes capture these gestures and fluctuating emotions. Here is an after-the-fact, easier-to-read version of the notes from our checklists and logs of a meeting between my client Principa and a Japanese firm—the negotiation mentioned in Chapter 5.

- Stan [one of the lead negotiators for the Japanese firm] feels that throughout the process we have been unprepared. Steve [also representing the Japanese firm] adds that they understood that we have a new salesperson, but he still categorizes us as "unresponsive."

So the Principa team is accused of being unprepared and unresponsive.

The noise has started.

- Stan names two issues (1) contractual agreement (CA) and (2) lack of commitment on our part. They believe that they've shown all the commitment to the project's goals—they talked about commitment at the corporate meeting—but we have not shown any. They state several times that they didn't know that our CA was required for the blueprint preparation to begin. They believe the commitments we made should override the need for the CA and we should agree to their work order.

So we lack commitment as well.

The volume is rising. The other side is trying to put the Principa negotiators under a lot of pressure.

- Mr. N. says they have put their jobs on the line for this project.

Now our failures in the negotiation have even jeopardized jobs on the other side.

Lots of emotions in the room right now, but the Principa negotiators stay calm.

- Mr. N states that *every vendor has accepted* their work order. *Every vendor* has understood that this is the way business is done with [this company] and with Japanese banks. He implies we're naïve about Japanese culture.

So we are unprepared, not responsive, and lack commitment—and now ignorant, stupid, and naïve as well.

- Stan goes on to highlight that maybe we don't understand who Mr. N is. He is a *very* important man in Japan. *Very* honorable. *Very* famous.

It is a shame we are so stupid! We listen calmly and keep writing as fast as we can.
They're screaming now.

- Steve says, while looking at Mr. N., that we are "unethical" and "unfair." Mr. N. agrees that we're definitely unfair.

Add unethical and unfair to the long list of Principa failings.
With this much noise, the pressure is really on.

- They abruptly leave. No hand-shaking.

They hope Principa will lose sleep, if not actually burn in hell, over our inexcusable behavior in this negotiation. That's the point of the abrupt departure.

I grant that this was a particularly rough session, but there's no denying that emotions can get out of hand in just about any negotiation, and one of your best ways to blank-slate and

control your own emotions, first, and then perhaps influence their emotions, by your example, is with the simple tool of taking notes. In this meeting, our note-taking did not succeed in modulating their aggressiveness, but it did succeed in keeping the Principa team under control. While you're taking notes, it's very hard to explode.

On the practical side, notes are documentation. How many times have you found yourself unable to remember a point? You have the gist of it, but not the specifics? Worse yet, when was the last time you found yourself trying to recall who said what, because you hadn't written down the names? Was it Sue or Sally? Jim or John? The "I'm not good with names" excuse doesn't cut it. And if you haven't even gotten the names right, what else have you forgotten or mixed up?

Here's a story. My clients John and Jeff, two brothers, were negotiating a consulting agreement with Louise and her team. The original idea was to hire Louise's team for twenty-four hours of consulting on eleven different topics. Louise quoted John and Jeff $48,000 for the entire job. In the course of four different conversations over three months, the number of hours and topics were reduced to fourteen hours and six or seven topics. Louise agreed that the price would be reduced at least proportionately, but in the end the final pricing would be driven by the total number of individual hours involved. No one on her team took any notes throughout these discussions. Louise's final proposals called for eighteen hours over two days, with ten topics to be covered. Her new quote was $42,000. Justin and Jason had taken notes. Louise had missed the number of hours and the number of topics, and she didn't even address the question of total number of individual hours. The discrepancies between the verbal agreement and Louise's proposal made my guys question her competence and capability. Or she was trying to gouge them. Either way, she was on the verge of losing this opportunity, and she didn't even know it. John and Jeff decided to call the owner of Louise's company, who immediately asked for a couple of days to resolve the issues. He asked the brothers if they would share their notes. Sure, and everything was eventually straightened out.

Well, you say, I'd never screw up the numbers like that. I hope you're right. If you take good notes, I know you're right.

Good notes are all upside. Good notes are the full story of the meeting. Most people can scribble down a few notes here and there in a conversation, but taking great notes takes lots of practice. Start with short and concise bullet points, which can be fleshed out later. Write down key words and who said them. Before the meeting or conversation ends, the wise course is often to go over them with the other side. No guessing later. Get straight right now what was said. If there's ever a time to 3+, this is it. There's no better way to make sure everyone leaves the meeting on the same page.

Test Drive It's so simple. The next meeting you go to, pull out your legal pad instead of your business card. The next time the phone rings, pick up your pen, really listen, and take notes, even if it's your mother on the line. (That might be the ultimate challenge, trying to blank-slate with a close member of your family.)

Test Drive Make a conscious effort to *not think* while someone is talking to you. Blank your mind and pay close attention to each and every word. *His or her* world, not yours.

SPILLING THE BEANS

Please don't spill your beans in the lobby. Let the other side spill theirs. That is, don't unwittingly reveal important information, and always be ready to scoop up such information.

Your spilled beans will get you in trouble sooner or later. Arthur had been recruiting a very talented young man to join his company at a high level. I had encouraged Arthur not to put forth a full financial package before he received a commitment from the candidate to reject or accept that package once it was offered. Why this stipulation? Well, without a commitment to reject or accept the offer, Arthur would get shopped by the recruit. If Arthur spills the beans, the recruit—if he is as good as Arthur believes—will take those beans and use them to negotiate with other firms, perhaps with his current firm, and Arthur would find himself in a bidding war. And that's exactly what happened, because Arthur declined my coaching on this point. His beans were the starting point, not the finishing point. He should have said, "We're going to commit to a financial package that will be at the top of the industry, but we're not going to reveal it until we have your commitment to reject or embrace our offer. We don't want this package to be used to start a bidding war with your current company." This is a fair approach, but companies are afraid they'll lose the candidate, so they spill the beans, and then they lose the candidate *because* they spilled the beans and the candidate uses the package to start an auction. This happens all the time.

My associate Phil and I were invited to preview a new invention and possibly join in the business venture bringing this product to market. At the meeting, we exchanged pleasantries and asked the obvious question, What can you show us? Three hours later, we had so much information we needed two trips to get it all to the car. We had not been asked to sign a nondisclosure agreement or a confidentiality agreement, yet we were driving away with all the information imaginable on this invention that could revolutionize how communities deal with water contamination. We had no intention of stealing this information, but what about the other people the inventors' team had given it to? I had bad visions of the possible consequences.

The eagerness to build vision for possible investors and partners had only thrown a blanket over our eyes. As negotiators, the inventors' team should have spent most of their time in Phil's and my world, of course. Discussing our interest in working with inventors and small entrepreneurial companies would have earned them much more initial interest. By getting into our knowledge of small business, they could have guided us to put together our thoughts on a potential business plan and effort. As it was, they scared us away. All the spilled beans served mainly to create a vision of an anxious group of businesspeople.

You might think that with written communication, beans would not get spilled as easily. But they do. Consider only "accidental" e-mails. How many times have you received an inadvertently forwarded e-mail that was not intended for your eyes? How many times have you sent or received the wrong version of a document—a wrong version with some intriguing differences from the official one? How many times has someone asked you a question in an e-mail and you've taken the opportunity to answer in great detail—too much detail, spilling the beans? I'm betting it has happened, because I make good use of e-mailed spilled beans almost every day.

Here's a surprise, or at least it surprised me in my early coaching days: Often enough, people will blatantly tell you they are about to spill some vital beans. They think they are helping their cause by giving up information, when in fact they are dramatically hurting it. I call these types unwitting agents.

> *You know I will do anything I can to keep our relationship on solid ground. I just don't want to see anything happen to it, so please keep this to yourself, but there is a little more discount available to you if you push a little harder. The executive committee approved it because of the importance of the relationship. So don't worry, push a little harder and you'll be looking at a great deal.*

Take that bean straight to the bank.

> *Please don't quote me, but I really like working with*
> *you and want you to know that there's lots of*
> *flexibility built into our budget. We've had a good*
> *year and have some breathing room. I can't say*
> *much more, but before you submit your proposal, if*
> *you have a specific question you think I can answer,*
> *just give me a call.*

That's not quite as flagrant a violation of the spilled-beans principle, but the net result should be just as good for you.

Why do people say these things? Why do they undermine their own negotiation? Neediness, as discussed earlier. They need to be important, they need to be okay, and they need to make a difference—or they are actually *planting* these beans, bogus information designed to build your expectations.

> *Susan would probably fire me for saying this . . . but*
> *the truth is that your product is right in line with*
> *her budget and technologically it's superior to the*
> *other bidders'.*

Is the informant spilling or planting beans? Find out. Always approach spilled beans gingerly. No expectations. No assumptions. Ask questions. Stay within your principles.

Throughout this book you've seen how negotiators use hints of big purchases, permanent alliances, and the like to set up naïve negotiators with neediness and positive expectations. I now add the point that those negotiators hope that one result of your positive expectations will be some spilled beans from you. *Say, Jeff, is that deadline you guys set really hard and fast?* Or maybe it's some remark that's just a little leading: *Boy, Jeff, that's an awfully close deadline you guys have in place.* Both enticements are in the hope that you, by way of friendship, and with your positive feelings about the negotiation, might slip and reply, *Well, you know how "deadlines" work, Paul. They have a way of coming and going.*

Too much talking, not enough listening. Too much talking, too many spilled beans. It's almost inevitable. As a negotiator, if you can't control the motormouth, you're eventually going to say something you'll regret for the duration of that negotiation. If you pay close attention to what they're saying, however, you will be the happy recipient of many spilled beans, because they couldn't control their own motormouths. Their own neediness seduces them into fighting to feel okay, fighting for their self-importance.

I am not going to kid you. It takes 24-hour discipline to let go of expectations, to guard against assumptions, to listen instead of talking, to take copious notes all the time, and to be cautious about needlessly divulging information. But with practice, blank-slating can become a behavioral goal and discipline you can control. You can make sure that your slate is erasable and easily adjusted. You will develop the habit of constantly reviewing the status of the negotiation. When your picture changes, you'll change with it. But even if you're disciplined and careful, the world outside the negotiation can still intrude on your ability to blank-slate. If you're overly tired, it's difficult to focus. If you're dealing with the remains of the night before, blank-slating is a chore. If there's a crisis in your home, blank-slating can be impossible. Therefore I say in all seriousness that if you feel you cannot blank-slate for any reason, you have only one option: Cancel the negotiating session. This is how important that blank slate is.

Test Drive
Before a negotiation, see that negotiation unfolding in your mind. Picture yourself asking the questions, taking the notes, and negotiating with all your tools honed to perfection. See yourself relaxed with no expectations, no assumptions, no need, and no fear—a perfect blank slate. The exercise helps, even for the veteran tough-as-nails negotiator.

Three-Minute Checklist

- Before the phone call, the e-mail, the meeting, take however long is required to assess your attitude and frame of mind.
- Those positive expectations, blatant or subtle: Are you aware of them? Have you put them aside?
- Those negative expectations: Are you aware of them? Have you put them aside?
- Any assumptions of any kind whatsoever?
- Now you're ready to talk less, ask questions, listen well, and find out what's going on.

9

Who's Calling the Shots?

Finding the Real "Decider"

Who's calling the shots? Who is the real "decider," as President Bush puts it? Who are the real decision-makers within the other bureaucracy? This might seem, at first glance, to be a fairly mundane issue, but it's a critically important issue in any negotiation. How can you create vision effectively without knowing who the decision-makers really are? You can't, so the decision-making process on the other side must be discovered and understood at the very beginning of the negotiation, or as soon thereafter as possible. As a rule, the bigger the organization, the more complex and confusing the decision-making process can be. When you're dealing with a corporation, winning the shell game can be as frustrating as any aspect of the negotiation. Now the decision-making is in this office, now in that one, now elsewhere.

> Just show me and I'll take it to the board.

> If I like it, I'll recommend it, and they always stamp my recommendations. It's just a formality.

> Just put your bid together based on the specs and I'll do the rest.

But it seldom works out this way, does it? In an e-mail, T.J. told me that Chris is the decision-maker, absolutely. If Chris says okay, it's a go. But when Chris does say okay, he adds that I really should meet with Lauren as well. In a large company, this kind of "bait and switch" is almost SOP, and not necessarily out of evil intentions on the other side. Think of the number of times you were, in theory, the sole decision-maker regarding a problem at work or at home, but ended up asking the opinion and approval of someone else. It may be no different for the negotiators across the table. Many times, an earnest negotiator doesn't even know the decision process in his company, not as it directly concerns this specific negotiation. The pathways can be complex, and they can change overnight. You will have to help this earnest negotiator figure it out.

Consider Chip, who was negotiating a new contract with the federal government to provide vehicle parts to our military establishment. His company had the business under an old contract that was about to expire. You can imagine the bureaucracy that must be conquered in order to sign such an agreement, and Chip was new to this account. He was assigned a procurement officer who duly issued the RFP, with which Chip complied. Over time, the negotiation became heated over price, and Chip told the procurement person that he was sorry but he could not lower his price. Okay, was the reply, we can't make you, but you will not be the supplier. There was only one problem with this gambit on the part of the procurement bureaucracy. Chip had done his research and found out that the only other competing supplier had dropped out—they couldn't handle the pricing demands.

So Chip held some cards in this negotiation! Told no, he requested a meeting with the civilian leader of procurement at the supply depot. The civilian leader reinforced the original "no" and also reiterated the point made by the first procurement person: Lower your price or lose the business. By this time, Chip knew that the supply of these spare parts, necessary for the war effort in Iraq, was becoming critically low. Chip was determined to find someone who could make the decision to pay the fair price.

He found a captain who sang the same old song. Chip asked him for permission to go to his superior. Granted—but he heard that same song again. This happened four more times. Finally, Chip was granted an appointment with an admiral at the Pentagon, who took a different position. *What! This purchase is being held up over that price disagreement?* Problem solved. Chip had finally found the decision-maker. Chip heard all those "nos" not because he had failed to build vision, but because budget constraints had limited the authority of the regular procurement bureaucracy. His predecessors on the account had settled for what they could get from that bureaucracy. Chip had done his research and decided to challenge it instead. The president of his company wishes Chip had been in charge of that account twenty years earlier.

The failure to find the decision-maker is a mistake I have seen committed umpteen times in all sorts of negotiations. At best, it means a waste of time, energy, and money. At worst, it means a failed negotiation, perhaps unnecessarily.

I know a company that was having a very difficult time trying to acquire a smaller company. I repeatedly asked the chief negotiator of the acquiring company, "What is driving this price?" He just didn't have a clue, and he's a really bright, diligent guy. He was convinced that the board of directors made the decisions, but we went down the list of possible decision-makers. Lawyers? No. Accountants? No. Heirs? Hmm. In small companies, they are often important shareholders. Who holds the largest block of stock and has most of the influence? He didn't know but he'd find out. The acquisition finally was resolved when it was discovered that the widow of the founder of the company was the vital decision-maker. Now brought into the loop, she revealed that the sale of her late husband's company represented, in her mind, the end of his legacy, and she was afraid he and his achievement would be forgotten. Her husband had been an inventor, and she was desperately trying to find a way to immortalize him, especially for her many grandchildren and great-grandchildren. Hence the inflated price until along came a buyer who would honor that legacy. One element of that purchase was a beautiful monument to the founder, the widow's husband.

Why do negotiators often fail to uncover the real decision-maker? One main reason, I believe, is that they fear they don't have the skills to negotiate with the *real* decision-makers. They actually know, even if only in the deepest recesses of their minds, that they're dealing with the wrong people. They know they're stuck with this nonpayside activity, but at least it's safe activity. Maybe they can even luck into a decision, any decision, and get the heck out. With the "No" system, however, you do have the skills to negotiate with *anyone*. No matter how elaborate the decision-making process, no matter how sophisticated the shell game played by the other side might be, you can handle it and find your way to the people who count. You simply *negotiate* each piece of the puzzle until you have the information you need. It's just that simple (if arduous).

Many times, the first person you deal with in a negotiation is little more than a messenger. You're expected to hand over your information, your proposal, and this individual will pass it on to people who count. In the old days, you might have complied. Now you won't. Now you understand that the moment you hand over your proposal, it belongs to—the messenger. It's totally out of your hands. You don't know if you can trust the messenger to do what he says he'll do. You don't know if the messenger is knowledgeable enough to effectively pass it on. You have no idea whether he's respected by the decision-makers, or whether he'll even get to them. Maybe his honest effort on your behalf will be sabotaged by others.

So what do you do when dealing with such a messenger? You negotiate an agreement regarding how your proposal will be passed along. This ensures that you stay involved in the decision-making process.

I have the job of handling this project. I'll take what you present to the others.

That sounds perfectly normal, Guy. What we try to do is help you in that presentation in any way we can. I'll be happy to make the presentation to you, and if it is not something you can support, just tell me and we will withdraw. On the other hand, if this is something you support, I will go with you to your colleagues and present the proposal and answer any question others might have. Is that fair?

It's fair, but what if Guy can't set up the meeting? What if he has been told from on high to find out what he can from you, and nothing more?

You know, I'm not sure who this will go to, or how high. My boss told me to see what's out there, so I called you to discuss this.

I'm glad you did, Guy. You've been put in a tough spot. But I can help you be successful with this. When could you and I meet with your boss?

Or what if you know that the decision will be made by a group, but your contact person is not even sure who's in that group?

I was given this assignment by the committee, but I don't really know who at the end of the day will be involved in the decision.

Well, the question is, Who should we invite to see what we're proposing? When could we meet with the full committee to figure this out?

What's happening here? You're protecting your proposal and also protecting Guy's okayness, which is vitally important to you. If Guy accepts your proposal, he will fight for it, or at least strongly support it with the higher-ups. This approach usually works. If it doesn't, if Guy never allows anyone else to take a proposal higher up, if he doesn't feel comfortable with you and is afraid the committee won't either, and will then blame him, you go to your second choice.

> *Guy, I understand that under no circumstance will anyone but you talk to the committee. All I ask is if you don't like what I show you, just tell me no and I'll get out of your hair. But if you like our proposal and wish to recommend it to the committee, all I ask is that you let me coach you on my proposal and what you might say. Allow me to wait out in the hall, just in case there are any questions the committee wants answered. That way you are protected with adequate information in case something unexpected comes up. Fair? That will be our deal.*

What if Guy won't go along? Go to your third choice.

> *Guy, I understand that no one is to be present during the committee meeting, even in the hall. All I ask is that you allow me to coach you on what to say, and if any question arises, allow me to wait in your office. You can call me there and I can provide you with any information you need. Of course, if you don't like my proposal today, it's okay; you won't hurt my feelings. Just tell me no and I'll go away. We'll take a shot at working with you next time around.*

If Guy still balks—unlikely, but always possible—you have to decide whether it's wise to continue further work here, because this situation doesn't look promising. How much have you put into this negotiation? Are you fighting too hard? Are you *needy*? Should you simply not allow your information to be shared without your participation? If you say no to Guy's demand, is there a chance he might discover he has made a mistake? Might he decide that you've been effective in your efforts and he should let you represent yourself? This situation could play out many ways. Whatever your decision, it will be a good one, because you have retained control of the negotiation and stayed within your principles. You have preserved the blocker's okayness. You've given him every opportunity to say no. You haven't tried to close him. You've given him every opportunity to have some vision. If you do decide to say no to Guy, you can always move in any other direction, because "no" is just the start of the negotiation, not the end. You could open up other fronts within Guy's organization. In this case, you may have to deal with Guy again, and he may not be happy with you for going around him, but you will have taken this possibility into account.

The talented negotiator moves freely within the decision process and even comes to enjoy solving the shell game. You eliminate all the wild cards you can think of. You continually ask yourself, Who's missing? Who's not in my loop? Who should be? You blank-slate. You do your research. You ask good questions. And be ready for unearthing multiple decision-makers, and be able and willing to negotiate with each and every one of them. This may not be the most glamorous aspect of the negotiation, but clearly, no decision-*maker*, no decision. (Recall the story with Chip and the military procurement bureaucracy. If Chip had decided to cave in on price, the lower echelons had the authority to sign off on the basic take-it-or-leave-it contract. They did not have the authority to negotiate, however. That was clear. So you can sign bad contracts without ever finding the real decision-makers, but you cannot sign good ones that way, much less the best ones.)

YOU'LL HAVE TO DEAL WITH BLOCKERS

In many, many instances, the biggest problem you'll encounter in this discovery process is someone on the other side— maybe even the initial messenger—telling you, assuring you, promising you, guaranteeing you that he is the decision-maker. But he's not. Why does this happen so often? Quite simply, this is yet another example of how we fight to be okay, and it's not okay to say, "I have to run everything past my branch manager."

It's no exaggeration to state that the decision-making process in an organization is *driven* by people's need to feel okay. When you walk into a reception area, what is the receptionist fighting for? The feeling of being okay. It's human nature! Who wants to feel powerless? Our big businesses are divided and subdivided into level after level after level: upper management, middle management, business development, engineering, legal, human resources—it's endless. People working in these big corporate environments often feel as if they're about to be swallowed up. They know they're replaceable, because they've seen companies plow ahead even when the boss quits abruptly and gets the (golden) parachute. People want to *mean something* in this bigger scheme of things, to make a beneficial difference, to feel okay. And a key way they can do this is by insinuating themselves into the decision-making process.

Once you have determined who the real decision-makers are, it may still be hard to get to them because of the "blockers" standing in the way. Beware of these sweet folks. *Always* show them respect, but don't buy into their game. Work diligently to circumvent their carefully guarded territory. The blocker could be the receptionist who screens the calls, or the executive assistant, or the co-manager, or, worst of all, the person you have incorrectly decided is the decision-maker. The apparent boss

can be blocking for the real boss. In one very complex negotiation, the real decision-maker was mentioned as a decision-
maker by everyone on the other side *except* those with whom
he directly worked. This guy turned out to be where the buck
stopped, and everyone in the division blocked for him.

In many companies, the purchasing office is one big
blocker. They handle the paperwork and not the decisions.
Everyone knows this. On more than one occasion my clients
have freed up a negotiation by removing the old team that
granted power to purchasing and bringing in a new team that
divorced itself from purchasing, putting that department
where it belongs in serious negotiations—out of the loop.

Disgruntled employers often turn into blockers. A particularly instructive story concerns the head of an evaluation
group who had been more or less displaced within his own
company. Colleagues had been promoted all around him. He
was standing still and didn't have a lot of positive feelings
about the situation. He was very defensive about every decision he had made in the past, and he was doing everything he
could to defend his decisions. Basic human nature. In addition,
one of his decisions had been responsible for an embarrassing
debacle for the company. So this man had a lot to defend and
was working as hard as he could to undermine any plans to get
around him. My clients finally succeeded, but not easily.

Fathers block for mothers, and mothers for fathers. The
teacher can be blocking for the principal. The city council can
be blocking for the mayor. If you can't identify and then go
around or over the blockers, you're in for a long, hard time, by
definition, because the blockers don't make the real decisions.

Always keep in mind that the boss in the corner office is
not necessarily the decider. I've mentioned President Bush,
who said he is the decider. Now I'll mention Abraham Lincoln.
During the Civil War, hundreds of individuals beseeched the
president himself—who else?—to make this appointment,
grant this clemency, and on and on and on. Yet time and again
they found out he couldn't or wouldn't make that decision, for

whatever reason. He would be overridden by the secretary of war, the secretary of state, his own private secretaries, his wife, General Grant, and many others more directly involved in day-to-day decision-making. This can be the case in any complex bureaucracy.

Do the blockers *think* of themselves as blockers? Sometimes yes, because they are under explicit instructions to block. Great leaders such as Lincoln surround themselves with great blockers who love the game. You can count on this. Often, however, blockers do not think in such terms. They just know what makes them feel okay. They are by nature defensive and believe that their job description is to obstruct forward progress, to create obstacles, and ultimately to thwart your endeavor. They may have other reasons for blocking as well. Their jobs might be on the line. They may be jealous, because you seem to be the decision-maker for your company, while they obviously are not for their own company; you're going to get a lot of credit or commissions or some kind of reward for this deal, while they're not. In short, what's in it for the blocker? Maybe not much.

IT NEVER HURTS TO START AT THE TOP

You can get around your basic blocker in several ways. One way is simply to start at the top. What happens if you start at the top? The top boots you down the ladder to a blocker, but this is fine, because, presumably, you've been introduced into the blocker's territory with a stamp of approval. The blocker knows it's okay to talk to you, and the blocker knows that you know that he is indeed a blocker.

Start at the top and you will be in a position to report to the top. You have a hall pass to the corner office upstairs. Blockers will therefore treat you with respect. If the CEO had time to talk to you, the blocker has time to talk to you. Or he had better find the time.

But all is not lost if you can't start at the top. You can still deal with the blocker from below.

Ring! Ring!

Hello, Dallas Cowboys, Tammy speaking.

Tammy, my name is John Harris and I need your help. I would like to know how best to approach Mr. Jones and Coach Parcels to become an offensive quality-control coach for the Cowboys. Should I send a résumé with a cover letter and letters of recommendation? Should I try to set up an appointment to speak with them? Who should I talk with first? I would appreciate any help you could give me.

Well, John, you should start by sending me a résumé with letters. I'll have them reviewed and get back to you.

Tammy, this means a great deal to me. Is there anything else I can do?

No, John, I promise you I will have your information looked over and get back to you.

May I call you and check in to see if there is anything else I can provide you?

Yes, John, that will be fine.

Thank you, Tammy. Good-bye.

What has John accomplished so far? By gaining instructions and an agenda from the blocker, he has a track to run on. Now the key will be how strong the résumé is, and how strong the letters of recommendation are. Will they create a strong positive vision? Will Tammy be impressed and feel okay taking John's application up the ladder?

Let's look at his follow-up call.

Ring! Ring!

Hello, Dallas Cowboys, Tammy speaking.

Hello, Tammy. This is John Harris. I spoke to you a week ago about my desire to be a quality-control coach with Coach Parcels on offense. I was hoping you had received my résumé and letters okay?

Why, hello, John. Yes, I did. In fact, I gave them to Coach Parcels and he said he would evaluate staffing after the Superbowl. Please call me then for an update.

Sounds easy, doesn't it? Maybe too easy. But it happens just like that every day. After all, it's just negotiation.

Three-Minute Checklist

- The shell game is not glamorous, but remember: No decision-maker, no decision.
- When dealing with messengers and blockers, always nurture. Be creative. Try again.

10

Getting What You Want

Building Your Success with Agendas

Each and every communication in a negotiation requires an agenda—and not just meetings where you're sitting across the table from the other side. Agendas are required even for telephone calls and e-mails. Maybe this sounds radical at first, but it's really not. You have some kind of purpose for every phone call and e-mail to anyone on the other side, right? I hope so. Well, what is it? The agenda makes this clear. The preparation of each agenda helps you see the negotiation clearly and assign priorities. If you're part of a team, agendas are absolutely crucial for keeping everyone on the same page in their various encounters with various people on the other team.

These agendas are different from those used by most negotiators and businesspeople. The typical agenda lists topics to be discussed, often in no particular order. Even if there is an order, we know what happens all too often: The anticipated order is more or less discarded and a free-for-all ensues. Your agendas can and must do better. And don't worry that preparing all these agendas will overwhelm you. In fairly short order, the preparation becomes second nature, and you will reap an incredible amount of control for a relatively small investment of time and energy. A good agenda will tell what to do next, how to keep your negotiation on track, how to continue making effective decisions, and how to keep your emotions at a calm, normal level.

AGENDA ESSENTIALS

A valid agenda has the following five basic categories.

- Problems
- Our baggage
- Their baggage
- What we want
- What happens next

The first three items are optional. They just may not be necessary for a given agenda. But "what we want" is a requirement for every agenda, because every e-mail, every phone call, every meeting entails something that you want to happen. "What happens next" is also a requirement for every agenda, because that's always the question, isn't it?

One final, critical point before we take a closer look at each category: The only valid agenda—the only agenda that will produce results—is the one that has been "negotiated" with the other side. Take a moment and be certain that you understand the implications here. In the "No" system, there are no hidden agendas, no surprises. What would be the point of one? You hope to get agreements that stick in the end by springing surprises? Hope again. Every element of the agenda must therefore be laid out clearly for the other side. You could even slide your agenda across the table for their careful consideration! Of course, you always provide every right to say no. You may well reiterate your points three times.

The more effective you are in presenting your agenda, the

more comfortable the other side will be. Your competence will be appreciated and *embraced.*

Let's see how each one of these items can help your negotiation.

PROBLEMS

For purposes of agenda, a problem is anything you believe needs addressing—anything you see that is holding you back or blocking you from a successful conclusion. A problem can even be imaginary—not really a problem at all, once it's examined—but the fact that it's imagined by one or both sides means that it's in the air, and if it's in the air it has to be dealt with. No matter how easy or difficult a problem may be, no matter how silly it might seem or how serious it actually might be, it must be dealt with, and therefore it has to be part of an agenda.

Sometimes both sides will fail to see a problem at first, or even for a long time, but more often negotiators are afraid to see problems—or they think they'll go away on their own, or they hope the other side won't see them and things will somehow work out. But negotiation doesn't work that way. Just recently we launched a training program with a new client that quickly began to go awry. Training sessions were canceled. Soon enough, the team was just not available—period. This was a problem, and we knew what to do. Place it on an agenda and negotiate. When we did this, it quickly became clear that an executive below the CEO did not want the program to be successful. The training had been the CEO's idea, but the team leader was uncomfortable with the discipline, accountability, and oversight. The CEO had seen this development coming but had decided to go ahead without addressing it, hoping to somehow overcome the opposition. But how could we continue the program if this problem was not dealt with?

A negotiation ensued, the problem was clearly defined, and a solution was found.

Not seeing problems is one thing, and will take care of itself, because the problems always surface. Trying to avoid them or finesse them in some way, as the CEO tried, is another issue. It never works. Don't even try. With problems, be preemptive, proactive, and all-inclusive.

Recall the meeting between Principa and the Japanese firm in Chapter 8, in which the other side got really aggressive and the Principa team sat calmly and took great notes. In the early weeks of that overall negotiation, the only problem the Principa team acknowledged and placed on their agendas was the lead negotiator for the Japanese firm. He was a problem and should have been on the agenda and dealt with as such. But the unwillingness of the Japanese firm to sign a contract was not on a single agenda prior to my arrival on the scene. When the biggest problem of all is not on the agenda—well, that's a problem! The negotiation was going nowhere, needless to say.

Every negotiation has its own set of problems, and you will find that many of them relate to the major principles of finding the real decision-makers, finding the mission and purpose, and, especially, building vision.

- Decision-Makers
  - We don't know with whom we should be talking.
  - We don't know who will be taking responsibility for this.
  - We don't know who sets disciplinary problems at the school.
  - We don't know who will invest the most time and energy in this.
  - We haven't talked with the entire committee to be sure we know how they will decide.

- Mission and Purpose
  - We haven't thought through exactly what we are bringing to this negotiation.

- ○ We have failed to think in terms of their world.
- ○ We made the mistake of not listing our features and benefits.
- ○ We didn't think enough about our responsibilities. We didn't do enough research to determine the true overall long-term aim.

- • Building Vision
  - ○ Our company doesn't know where your company is going with its new program, and therefore we don't know what issues or challenges to address for your team.
  - ○ Our company doesn't know what your challenges are. We don't know what the end user truly requires. We can't respond to a request for proposal without a thorough understanding of the issues at the end-user level.
  - ○ As a teacher at this school, I want to put our recent problems at the school right out front, so you can see our solutions and are comfortable with what we've done.
  - ○ Mr. Jones is being pressured for a decision, and we haven't taken the time to help him see what can be accomplished. We're failing to help him see what can be done.
  - ○ We have not done a good job of creating a unified vision of the challenges they face. We're getting conflicting direction from different departments of their company.

When you deal with problems head-on, the other side sees you as effective. This is comforting for them, of course, and it helps your own self-esteem. A straightforward way to test your progress in negotiation is to evaluate how well you work on solving the most difficult of problems in your negotiations. If you are digging deep to find and then solve the real problems, you are well on your way to owning this system of negotiation.

A final, crucial point: This digging for problems must start with a close appraisal of yourself. When your behavior and activity mistakes are not dealt with, you are the problem. Face the music and put it on an agenda.

"I put too much pressure on you. I actually screwed up your opportunity. I apologize. That won't happen again."

"I have fallen short in my engineering of this solution. It's that simple."

Likewise, look closely at your team. Sometimes problems caused by team members are obvious, sometimes not. Steve was a representative with a manufacturing firm that supplies a Fortune 100 company. He was dealing with a very tough procurement group and was losing his respect for them. This attitude was beginning to show in his behavior. He was smarting off during meetings. He wasn't bothering to ask good questions. And the negotiation was going nowhere. All this was discovered when Steve's team leader took a look at Steve's own notes, which were full of nasty asides. Steve's attitude was a problem. Solution: Replace Steve and put his bad attitude on the agenda for the next meeting with the other side. Problem solved.

We negotiators are the problem so often that I have a rule:

Look first to yourself and your team as the root of the problem.

When the problems seem insurmountable, you may give up. If you do, you become the real problem underlying the other problems, because you don't deal with them head-on. Think of it this way: If you don't address each and every problem, you'll never come to an agreement, almost by definition. If you do address each and every one, you have a chance . . . a good chance . . . an excellent chance of gaining an agreement that lasts. So that's your choice with problems.

Test Drive   Regarding a recent negotiation, list all the "problems" that cropped up—all of them, including the ones that you wouldn't have given that label in the beginning. Now check off those problems that might *conceivably* have been rooted in your own attitudes and actions. I believe you'll end up with some check marks.

BAGGAGE—YOURS AND THEIRS

My guess is you've never made an agenda that included *baggage*, the collected life experiences and observations that all of us carry around in our lives and that may affect a given negotiation. You have undoubtedly worked your way through a lot of your personal baggage in all realms of your life—all of us have—but vigilance is always called for. Brand-new baggage can pop up at any time! How many negotiations have been hindered by issues relating to gender, age, appearance, financial status, experience, seniority, and a lot more? Many of them, maybe even most. When baggage isn't addressed, when it lurks below the surface, how can everyone at the table talk openly? It's hard. How can everyone get past the emotions that the baggage stirs up? With great difficulty. How can everyone make clear-eyed decisions? It's almost impossible. This is why you must deal with whatever baggage you think might conceivably interfere in the negotiation. Put it on an agenda.

The line between "problems" and "baggage" is a thin one, and not critical. I separate them mainly in order to give you *two chances* to identify all possible candidates. Use your imagination, use your experience, and use your common sense. When in doubt, err on the side of including any and all possible baggage (as well as problems) on an *early* agenda. Baggage addressed and discarded by all concerned is not a problem; baggage that isn't discarded becomes an intractable problem.

Your Baggage   Your baggage is some attitude you carry around that plays on your emotions and disrupts your decision-making. Say your company has recently acquired a reputation within the field, or within the community, for spotty bad service. This is nasty baggage. It must be addressed in an early agenda. That's right. *You* bring it up, with two instant benefits. First, they'll be surprised and impressed that you haven't tried to hide the fact. Second, if unaddressed, that baggage puts you on the defensive for the entire negotiation. It primes you to make all kinds of compromises. So put your recent reputation on the table—along with (I hope) declarations that you have solved these service problems.

More possible baggage for you:

- They once pulled a fast one and gave me used parts instead of new ones. I have a negative attitude going in.
- I'm convinced that Johnny's teacher thinks my child is the main disruptive force in his classroom.
- They charged us 30 percent more than they charged Acme. I'm angry about that.
- The former crew definitely did not like taking orders from a woman. I know this is a new crew, but being a woman, I'm still leery.
- They lied about the requirements and hurt our other deal. I remember that well.
- They talk about us in a very negative way to our clients. We have to get this straight.
- They think my age [all of thirty-eight!] prevents me from keeping up with this new field, which seems to change overnight, every night.

Their Baggage

Their baggage is an educated guess on your part. You'll be making an assumption dealing with baggage, and this is the only time an assumption is warranted. Maybe you're wrong, but past history gives you good reason to bring it up. After all, your job is to eliminate assumptions, and what better way than to bring them to the forefront and deal with them? This may be difficult to do, but you should be more afraid of the baggage that is neither recognized nor negotiated in the beginning.

- They think we're too small. I don't think they will work with us because of that perception.
- They think our fumble with the last order is the way we do business—period. They'll cancel this order the first chance they get.
- Apparently they don't believe in paying full invoice price. Why should they this time?
- I've been told they are hard to work with and will do everything in their power to make us fail.
- They are suspicious regarding how we can quote a price three times lower than the closest other bidder.
- Their design group just doesn't like us. They never have—for no reason we can figure out. Given that, how can we possibly expand our role within their company?
- This homeowner has been suspicious about everything I've done on this job. He's convinced I'm cutting every possible corner. I don't know why, but that attitude is undermining our relationship.

I was working with a new client, George, who like most new clients was eager to make assumptions about what the other side was thinking, what the other side was doing or going to do, and of course what the other side would think. George and his team were involved with a negotiation in which they had already lowered their price twice and were on their way to offering a third discount. I got involved at this point and began by asking George what he saw as the real problem dragging down the negotiation. His answer went like this: "Well, I think they are afraid to tell us no and have gone to other suppliers to bring back into the deal. I also think this comes from their culture. I read that in their culture they don't have a word for 'no.' So instead of telling us no, they have just turned their backs on us and have not responded to our last request. They have gone another direction and now we are out."

Now go back and take a look at George's baggage. Look where all his assumptions have taken him—all the way from they're afraid to tell us no to we're completely out of the picture now. Imagine the effect these assumptions would have on this negotiation if allowed to just lie there. You can see what they would do to George's decision-making. More compromise!

Dealing with baggage will *not* be resented. The other folks weren't born yesterday. They'll know where you're coming from and respect you for asking. Or maybe the baggage you lay on the table *does* kill the deal then and there. Say you're new to the field, and say the other side just won't take seriously anyone who's still paying dues. So what's the loss if you lay your inexperience on the table and the other party walks away? You weren't going to get anywhere anyway. But if the other party does *not* walk off, you have gained a great deal of respect for forthrightness and competence that will go a long way toward offsetting your inexperience, and you have negotiated a track on which to run without being blindsided.

Baggage destroys many a negotiation, because negative emotions often come from baggage. It makes vision just about impossible. It always impairs decision-making.

**Baggage is as bad as it gets. Deal with it or
you'll get nowhere.**

WANTS

Too often people go into meetings not sure exactly what they want out of them. Your agenda solves that problem for you, because every agenda for every meeting, every phone call, every e-mail must have at least one "want." No exceptions. The "want" requirement for every agenda requires you to think clearly about the whole negotiation—where it stands and what you want to happen next in order to move things along. And if you're unable to articulate what you want at every point in a negotiation—well, this tells you a lot, doesn't it? Stop, step back, and figure it out.

Without this clear understanding and picture of what you want at every step in a negotiation, you can't put it on an agenda. If you can't put it on an agenda, you have no right to ask for it. And if you can't ask for it, you put yourself completely at the mercy of the other side. You'll be buffeted by noise and, perhaps, obfuscation. So if you want to stay in control to the greatest extent possible—and you do—what you want must be a part of every agenda.

What does every "want" entail from the other side? A decision, of course. From a phone call to set up a meeting, you want a decision about the time and place for the next face-to-face meeting. From the face-to-face meeting, you want a decision on whether you can submit a proposal. And so on. These wants all require a decision on their part. Decisions are good, even if the decision is "no"! Progress depends on real decisions, not a bunch of "maybes." Therefore, I'd like you to consider each "want" in the negotiation in terms of the decision required on the other side in order to fulfill it. You want the other side to reject or accept what you want. You want them to make a decision to move the negotiation forward. Look at these examples.

Your want:
You want a meeting to discuss the latest changes in your proposal.

The same want asking for a decision:
You want them to reject or accept a meeting to discuss the latest changes in your proposal.

Your want:
You want the termite report.

The same want asking for a decision:
You want them to either refuse to submit the termite report or to submit it.

Your want:
You want the teacher to see that you are making every conceivable sacrifice to support Danny's education.

The same want asking for a decision:
You want to know whether the teacher agrees that you're doing your very best at home to support Danny's work in the classroom.

Identifying "wants" and the decisions they call for seems so easy on paper. Often it's not in practice. Here's what can happen when you aren't clear about what you want:

> "John, I have an idea for your business that could increase its value dramatically."
>
> "Good, Bill. Let's see it."
>
> "Great, John. I'll lay it out right here on the desk."

Ten minutes later . . .

> "I like what I see, Bill. Let me study it for a week or two, then get back to me."
>
> "Sure, John. I'll talk to you in a few weeks."

What did Bill *want* in this negotiation? From that conversation, no one would know. What was the outcome? Unfortunately, this we do know: Poor Bill has spilled his beans and is now completely at the mercy of John. In fact, he's running the risk of having John take the new idea to a third party, maybe even slipping himself into the deal as broker of record. Insult and injury!

How could Bill's negotiation with John have been structured to keep Bill in control? First, he has to ask himself what he wants at this earliest stage of the negotiation. What he wants—or should want—is to protect his ideas. The following would have been a productive approach:

> "John, if I had an idea for your business that could increase its value dramatically over the next five years, who would be involved in the decision process?"

> "Bill, I make all those decisions."

> "Of course you do, but who would give you good advice in financial areas?"

> "Well, Bill, I'm the guy, but I would want my attorney and tax man to look at it."

> "I see, John. Who else would you get involved?"

> "No one else; that would be the group."

> "John, here is what I'd like you to do. I have an idea drawn up. I'd like to show it to you. If you like it, can you and I show it to your attorney and accountant together? Of course, if you don't like it, we'll drop it. Fair?"

> "Sounds fair to me."

> "Okay, John, our deal is that if you like my idea, we'll go together to see the attorney and the tax man. Please sign this 'broker of record' to protect my ideas. This says that others can't take my ideas and use them without my being paid. Are you comfortable with protecting my work?"

> "Sure, I have no problem with that. If you do the work, you get paid."

> "Are you sure you're okay with this?"

> "I have no problem with it, Bill. It's only fair. Here's my John Hancock."

By asking a few questions of himself and determining exactly what he wanted from that meeting with John, Bill was able to negotiate an agenda over which he could have some control. Of course, this doesn't mean he'll get the deal. He still has difficult negotiations ahead. But at least he has a chance to get things off on the right foot.

But what if John won't sign the proposed agreement? Well, find out now. If you know from the beginning what you want, there is no need to compromise unnecessarily and no danger of being surprised or blind-sided later.

> **Of all the issues in the negotiation that should be placed on an agenda but often are not, "wants" are supreme.**

If you can't figure out what exactly you want at a given point in the negotiation, some other element of your system must be a little out of whack. Is your mission and purpose in place? Have you done your research? Do you understand how to build their vision? Are your emotions under control, your baggage front and center? Maybe not. Or maybe you're chasing results and rushing to close and are therefore unable to slow down and think things through, step by careful step.

If you don't know what you want, something is not right, that's for sure. If you don't know what you want, how effective can you be not just in this particular meeting, but in the negotiation in general? What's the point in proceeding, really? You're just wasting your time and theirs. On the other hand, knowing what you want out of each stage of the negotiation—what you want on each agenda—helps you make sure that your mission and purpose is clear. It guarantees that your goals are clear. It makes you think clearly how to proceed—A, B, C, D, E, and all the way to Z and a deal that sticks.

Knowing what you want will make you "rich" in agenda. You can make all the negotiating mistakes in the world, but if you get a handle on what you want and get these wants placed on an agenda, you've got a chance.

Test Drive Sit down and think about a "typical" negotiation in your field—if there is such a thing—and draw up a list of the "wants" that are likely to pop up along the way. You may be surprised how long this list is.

Test Drive Take the list you generated in the preceding test drive—a typical list of "wants" in the typical negotiation in your field—and rephrase it as a question that requires a decision from across the table. By framing your wants in terms of those decisions, you discipline yourself to live in their world— a theme of the entire "No" system, of course.

WHAT HAPPENS NEXT

The last agenda item is "what happens next." How many times have you been in a negotiation and assumed that when the other party said "Call me back," they really meant it, but when you did call they were busy and couldn't talk? How often is a brush-off like "I'll talk to you in a few weeks" accepted by a negotiator who gets sucked into small talk, gets uncomfortable, leaves the subject, makes assumptions, and doesn't conclude business? It happens all the time, because you get lost in the emotion of the final moments of a meeting or phone call. But you must learn very quickly to take care of business by carefully negotiating "what happens next." It protects you against assumptions. It's a leg up on the next agenda. It's simply mandatory.

One last rule about agendas: The only agenda that is valid for purposes of negotiation—the only agenda that will produce results—is the one that has been negotiated with the other side. Take a moment and be certain that you understand the implications of this rule:

Joe, I'm not sure this information has any value to you, and if it doesn't, just say so and we'll go no further. Fair? Okay. Then that's our agreement. If it doesn't apply, that's that. If it does apply, we'll move forward, okay?

With this agenda in place Joe isn't going to feel blind-sided or pushed to close. You've given him every right to say no. You've reiterated your point three times (3+). Your own emotions are under control. That's a valid agenda. The more effective you are in negotiating the agenda, the more comfortable the other side will be in allowing you into the inner sanctum. Your competence will be appreciated and *embraced.*

ENOUGH SAID

No more explaining. Let's walk through a couple of agendas together. I'll set the scene and then create the agenda.

Judy is a freshman in high school. She has always maintained excellent grades in math, but now her first weeks of algebra have left her completely confused and afraid of failure. She cries every morning before going to school. Her teacher, Mr. Jones, tells her she just needs to work harder. She does so at home and stays after school for extra help, but Mr. Jones is never available. When she reports this last fact to her parents, they become very concerned and want a new math teacher for Judy. They request an immediate meeting with the principal, which is granted. Here is a good agenda for that meeting, from the parents' perspective:

PROBLEM: Judy is not getting the help she needs in math.
OUR BAGGAGE: Terrible fear of failure that could affect her future college opportunities.
THEIR BAGGAGE: We're concerned that Mr. Jones is too busy to provide help and support.

WHAT WE WANT: We want everyone to reject or embrace the proposal that a new teacher is required and that a tutor should be hired to help Judy.

WHAT HAPPENS NEXT: If everyone agrees, Judy is immediately transferred and a tutor is hired. Otherwise the next step is another meeting with Mr. Jones.

Another example:

Jason is a small-business owner who has a very creative team of designers who work well together. Cathy, a key member of this team, is talking of leaving in the near future. Jason would like to keep her. She is an instrumental part of the team and a key factor in the overall success of the project. Here's Jason's agenda:

PROBLEM: I have no idea why Cathy is talking about leaving.

OUR BAGGAGE: I have bent over backwards to help Cathy thrive in her work. I need to let that go. Clearly, my good intentions haven't helped Cathy.

THEIR BAGGAGE: I have no idea.

WHAT WE WANT: For Cathy to agree or disagree to share her vision of what is leading her away.

WHAT HAPPENS NEXT: Find out what would help her to stay.

And one more:

Mark has an interview for a job he really wants. He has been studying and attending various training programs for the last three years to qualify. There are more than thirty applicants for one position. Mark's agenda:

PROBLEM: I don't know what challenges the company and its leadership face.

OUR BAGGAGE: I'm needy. I feel that all of my hard work over the past three years must pay off. I have to let that go.

THEIR BAGGAGE: No idea.

WHAT WE WANT: For them to share their vision of their challenges they would like solved.

WHAT HAPPENS NEXT: Another interview to move the negotiation forward.

The logic is simple: By crafting agendas, you find out where you stand. By putting these agendas into action, you *improve* this standing.

Three-Minute Checklist

- Do you have an agenda for this phone call or this meeting?
- Has this agenda been negotiated with the other side? It must be.
- Does this agenda include, at a minimum, "what you want" and "what happens next"? It must.
- Does it include problems and baggage? If they exist, it must.

11

Managing the Real Price
Being Paid

Budgeting Beyond Dollars and Cents

I n the "No" system, the budget is much more than your normal itemization of projected financial costs, because the *real* price and the *real* costs in any negotiation go way beyond dollars and cents. Money is certainly part of the equation, but your budget must also take into account expenditures of time, energy, and emotion. Along with money, they are the elements of a comprehensive budget that becomes another powerful tool for maintaining control and making good decisions in negotiation.

The individual components are inextricably linked—a series of dominoes. "Time is money" happens to be true in negotiation. Time is also emotion: As the investment of time mounts higher and higher, so does the psychological and emotional pressure to make decisions. Money also brings emotion into the picture. In short, drive up any one budget item and you drive up all of them. The danger in any negotiation is that you become overinvested in budget. One element starts getting out of control—time, say—and the other three soon follow. What happens then? You probably lose sight of your mission and purpose. You probably start chasing results you can't control. Bad behavioral habits creep into the picture: You don't blank-slate, you can't figure out your agenda, and you lose patience with building vision. Neediness is suddenly in charge, and you start thinking, *Well, I've already invested so much here, I have to get something out of it.*

This is the classic logic that inevitably yields bad decisions and bad deals. But if you understand and keep track of your budget, it never has to happen to you. Never. Budget is the only way to take into careful account these four factors that are so important and yet so often overlooked as a total package that can undermine any negotiation.

Clearly, expenditures of time, energy, and emotion are not quantifiable in the way money is. You don't run out of them in quite the same way as you may run out of money. How, then, do you know when you've overinvested your budget—when you've reached your limit and can spend not one more dime, not one more minute, not one more fit of anger, and not one more breath on this ill-fated negotiation? It's a judgment call on your part, a call based on your experience and on your mission and purpose. In order to help you make this call, I have devised a rough-and-ready formula that drives home the *relative* importance of each of these budget items in your *overall* budget. As the negotiation proceeds, you monitor the expenditure in each category. You monitor your overall expenditure. You make good decisions based on what you see.

Here is the formula: "Time" has a value of 1x, "energy" 2x, "money" 3x, and "emotion" 4x. As important as time is, it is not as important as energy in negotiation, which is less important than money, which is less important than emotion. Again, you can't monitor numbers for these categories, because those numbers don't exist. You monitor these *relative* relationships.

Let's say you agree to meet with a prospective widget supplier. You spend thirty minutes with the new people, inspect their widget, and ask good questions. So you've invested some time and some energy, but not much of either. Time is money, yes, but you've spent so little time that the money is negligible. Likewise the energy, and you have no emotional investment in this young negotiation with the new supplier. You have no neediness because you're perfectly happy with your current widget supplier. It's no problem if you never see these people again—so you feel. Therefore your total budget is 1x for time × 2x for energy, for a total budget of 2x. No problem. You might even agree to meet with them again, if you're intrigued by their widget or believe you might have some price leverage with these upstarts.

Okay, you do meet with them again. This time you see some superior qualities in their widgets. Pricing isn't clear yet, but it seems that it will be roughly competitive. You decide to move ahead, take another meeting, and visit the new widget factory on the other side of the state. Now you're getting into a time-and-energy territory that translates into some real money, as well as actual cash outlay for the travel. Now your budget range is 1x for time × 2x for energy × 3x for money. Total: *6x*. With money in the game, suddenly your negotiation has tripled in value, from 2x to 6x. Again, we're not talking numbers here. We're talking about your judgment of your overall investment in budget.

Now let's say that you've decided that this is a better widget. That's all there is to it. In the beginning you didn't care about it, but now you do, because it could help you on the line. (The other side has done a good job of building your vision.) Because it's better, this widget is probably going to be a little more expensive. This hasn't been nailed down, not by a long shot, but it's looking that way. You'd live without the widget, sure, but you'd like to have it. In fact, you're feeling a touch of neediness. You're getting a little excited. Now you're almost afraid of losing this opportunity. In short, you have now invested some emotion in this negotiation, and emotion is worth 4x in your budget. Multiply the old preemotion total budget of 6x times 4, giving you 24x. This is an exponentially larger number. I have set up my formula in this way for a reason: When the

emotions try to kick in, watch out. Your overall budget mush-
rooms. This does not mean that you pull back from the negotiation. Not at all. It does mean that you proceed with care. You
negotiate on price and quantity. You build their vision of what
such a sale to you could mean to them. You don't jump up and
agree to any price they ask for. In short, you stay within your
system, helped by the constant monitoring of your budget.

ADVANTAGEOUS BUDGETING

As you monitor your own budget expenditure, you also monitor the expenditures of the other side.

> **You want to keep your own budgets as low as
> possible while reaping the benefit of higher
> budgets on the other side.**

Is building the budget on the other side just gamesmanship? Not at all. It's a valuable way to get their attention—to
push their vision of the issues. Negotiators dillydally, play
games, and in many other ways simply aren't serious. These folks
need your help in order to push forward to serious decision-
making. One way you do this is by building their budgets,
which then focus the attention marvelously. Ho Chi Minh just
kept building and building and *building* the Americans' budget
in Vietnam—time, energy, money, and emotion (as registered
by the American electorate as the number of combat fatalities
passed 10,000 . . . 20,000 . . . 30,000 . . . 40,000 . . . *50,000*). Think
about it: Building the Americans' budget in the jungles of Vietnam *and* over the negotiating table in Paris was the best way
for the North Vietnamese leaders to build our vision of our ultimate problem, which was that this war was never going away
unless we were willing to level North Vietnam in order to save
South Vietnam, and we weren't.

No, building budgets definitely is not gamesmanship. It's integral to building vision for the other side as quickly as possible (which was not very quickly in Vietnam).

Practically speaking, how do you drive up the other side's budget and guard yours? Some budget-building ploys are transparent. The use of time against you can start with something as common as your trying to get an appointment. When the other side requests you to do more preparing, gathering critical research, traveling, executing, and debriefing, simply say no. If you are monitoring your budget, you'll know when enough is enough.

Protecting your time while pushing theirs can be in acts as mundane as adhering to a schedule that fits your calendar and not theirs. You return phone calls based on your schedule. You don't leave long messages; therefore *they* have to call you back. If someone asks you to forward him or her an e-mail, fine, but on your schedule. My clients love to hear from the other side "Okay, let's cut to the chase," because this may mean that the other side has spent their time-and-energy budget and are suddenly seeing the issues very, very clearly and are finally willing and able to make an effective decision.

Remember the negotiation between the air-conditioning company based in the Southwest and the company building the cell phone network for the Middle East? As part of the foreign company's campaign to pry ridiculous price discounts and exclusive rights out of our client, they played all the tricks in the book. They set false deadlines and missed scheduled calls. They demanded due diligence and then still more due diligence. They changed certain technical requirements, then changed the new ones. They kept the real decision-makers under wraps and unavailable. They broke promise after promise. All of this activity and behavior was transparently intended to drive up my client's budget across the board, drive up his neediness, wring out every last concession.

None of it worked with him. None of it should work with you, because your mission and purpose is your *long-term* aim— your *continuing* task and responsibility. Properly monitored and managed, time actually becomes your ally. It is there to work for you, not to "run out" on you. Budgeting time is a matter of discipline, of maintaining patience, of following mission and purpose with dedication and skill. If these are handled well, the time-on-the-calendar question takes care of itself. Time can be wasted in a one-hour negotiation. It can be utilized to the fullest in a *one-year* negotiation. Time spent tells us nothing about time *well* spent. If your time is well spent, you have "all the time in the world" for this particular negotiation. If it's not well spent—and only you know—be ready to walk away.

In your personal life, you make time-and-energy budget decisions every day. Is this particular battle with adolescent Janie worth the time? Do you have the energy, or will you conserve your strength for what may be a more important showdown next week? Such budget decisions are at the heart of every parent's life. The credit card company definitely screwed up—or is pulling a fast one with the fine print, one way or the other. You do not owe that $30 fee, but do you have the budget required to obtain justice? Is this fight worth it? You may decide it's not. The average busy American probably makes dozens of such budget calculations every week without even really thinking in these terms. In your negotiation life, you need to think in these terms. When was the last time someone asked, "May I have a few minutes of your time?" and you granted this time. This was basic courtesy, which is great, but by doing so you unwittingly placed little or no value on those minutes, correct? You didn't know what the agenda was. You were just being nice, but when enough such unsolicited, unwanted time-eating episodes pile up in the day—answering e-mail will come to mind for many of us; it certainly does for me—a considerable amount of time is down the drain by day's end. The negotiator must carefully consider the value of his or her time.

All time spent represents energy, of course, and driving up your time with bogus assignments can't help but drive up your energy budget. But tough negotiations may require an expenditure of energy well beyond just the time required. This is when your disciplined system is mandatory, because keeping your needs in check, forgetting goals you cannot control, concentrating on actions and behavior you can control, and constructing good agendas—all the principles of the "No" system—are, in the end, a way for you to save energy.

Invalid, pointless appointments and meetings? A waste of energy. Accepting "maybe" for an answer? A waste of energy. Accepting an early "yes" for an answer? A waste of energy. Running from "no" as an answer? A waste of energy. Asking questions that don't do you any good? A waste of energy. Failing to blank-slate and making assumptions instead of doing valid research? A waste of energy. *Needing* something? A terrible waste of energy.

The old adage "penny-wise, pound-foolish" is right on. Skimping on preparation and research in order to hold down your time and energy budgets is the ultimate in "penny-wise, pound-foolish" behavior. Don't kid yourself. This isn't conserving energy. This is laziness, which is a terrible waste of energy and everything else in the budget, sooner or later, when your lack of preparation causes the whole negotiation to go south.

What's the cumulative impact of excessive time and energy expenditure? You're more than tired. You're totally spent. Which is to say, you're totally vulnerable. In negotiation, the physically stronger, more energetic side definitely has the advantage. It's a fact of life in this world. Know your own endurance level and conserve your energy. Don't hesitate to take a break from an hour-long meeting, call time-out during a round-the-clock negotiation, or even stand down for a week during protracted negotiations. It does you no good to make decisions when you're dog-tired. You don't want the agreement that will result from that fatigue. So . . . time-out.

Budget is yet another way for you to maintain control in negotiation. If your budget gets out of control, you cannot blame the other side.

Some quipster once said, "When they say it's not about money, *it's about money.*" Indeed. Once you and the other side start flying around the country and spending real money during the negotiation, once you get serious about exchanging much more money when the agreement is signed, the value of the negotiation goes up dramatically. Remember, time is 1x, energy 2x, money 3x, relatively speaking. Money matters boost a modest 2x negotiation to 6x status. If you are constrained by money and the other side is not, watch out.

I guess the most obvious example is a lawsuit pitting a solo practitioner against a large corporation. Legal proceedings are not, technically speaking, negotiations, since they're regulated by legal factors that don't affect true negotiations, but my point stands: The corporation is in a position to drive up the freelancing lawyer's dollars-and-cents budget past the point of endurance. It's not a fair fight, in this regard, and money talks in lawsuits. It talks in true negotiations. Whether you're a lawyer of a supplier or provider of service of any sort, you have to find out how the corporation operates in its dealings with smaller companies and solo professionals. Wouldn't you want to know if the individual or company on the other side has the reputation of driving up money budgets by insisting on meetings all over the country, maybe even the world? This tactic of driving up the dollars-and-cents budget of their smaller suppliers is also a basic strategy for the purchasing departments of the big multinationals, who are essentially immune from many money constraints of their own. The party to the negotiation that feels the money squeeze is under terrible pressure to compromise. A rock-solid faith in mission and purpose will be required in order to hold the line, but even then you simply may not have the budget to back you up in this negotiation. Know your actual dollars-and-cents budget, and have at least some sense of theirs. If you don't have enough cash reserves for the long haul, your negotiation is, for all intents and purposes, over with before it even gets going, and you'll lose not only the money but the time, energy, and emotion you have invested in a doomed cause. So don't even get going. Seek your deals else-where. Say no right now.

Time, energy, and money add up quickly enough. When emotions come into play, the budget can skyrocket immediately. 1x (time) $\times$ 2x (energy) $\times$ 3x (money) $\times$ 4x (emotion) equals *24x*. The excitement of winning and the pain or fear of losing, of failing, are the two key emotions that stand ready and able to sabotage both you and the other side. Several times we have seen how sophisticated corporate negotiating teams are trained to drive up the neediness and therefore the emotional budget of their would-be suppliers and providers with promises, threats, ridiculous requests, deadlines, and sudden exclamations that all is lost. It's a ruthless game, but it can be countered. You control your needs, your positive and negative expectations, your fears, your ego, your responses, and your decisions. Good, solid discipline is required, frankly, but that discipline is now within your reach. These are the last results you would ever chase, because you are wise to the ways of these big-time corporate negotiators. You stay within your system. This is all the armor you need. In the matter of budget, you work to build their vision, their expectations, and their fears.

JUDGE FOR YOURSELF

Quite a few years ago, one of my very best students, Jerome, was conducting what was shaping up as the largest negotiation in the history of his rather small company, which I will call Bonita, Inc. It was long, difficult, and expensive, to say the least—certainly by Bonita's standards. (At that time, its largest deal had been for $1.2 million. This new one might come in at something over $9 million.) The other company was considerably larger. I call it the Lancelot Corp. As I lay out this negotiation between my man at Bonita and Lancelot, look at it in terms of budget—time, energy, money, and emotion. There are many great lessons here, but focus on budget.

Bonita's upper echelon studied the prospects for this deal and determined that there was an adequate budget for the negotiation. They would invest the resources—and not just in money terms. Given the green light, Jerome burned the midnight oil structuring his mission and purpose and his goals and objectives, and doing his research. He struggled. He lost sleep. His time and energy budgets grew apace. At a certain point, money kicked in. Preparation for this negotiation was just about all Jerome was doing. He was practically on a leave of absence from the rest of the business at Bonita. As the weeks and then months passed, the company's commitment to the project grew, and soon the boss was putting the fate of the company in Jerome's hands: *We're counting on you; you're the guy; you're the man; you're the only one who can pull this off.* So add emotion into the budget mix. He was at the 24x level.

As Jerome's budget grew, problems arose. Colleagues were getting in the way. They said they wanted Jerome to win, but they were also afraid he would, because his success would threaten them. At the very least, it would put pressure on them to perform at his level. He needed their support, and they pledged to be there, but the work came in poorly executed and late, or not at all. Burned once too often, Jerome was now afraid to let anyone else get involved. He was beginning to feel very alone. The meetings with the Lancelot teams (plural) intensified. Jerome was working with dozens of different agendas at a time. The energy he was spending was the energy that was driving him forward, and he was doing a great job. Presentations were mandatory with Lancelot, and Jerome made over a dozen solid presentations to various teams at Lancelot, and he heard a firm and welcome "no" almost as many times. Jerome could smell victory. He prepared to make what he thought might be the final presentation. (He was tempted to hope that it would be the final one, but that hope would be an assumption, so he put it forcefully aside.)

After all this, the boss called Jerome in and said, "I'm awfully proud of you, but I've decided to take over the negotiation myself now." The man in the corner office was stepping in. Jerome was no longer required. Unbelievable, but what could he do? Did he perhaps feel just a touch of relief? (He was off the hook, after all. He had done his share and a lot more.) Not a chance. He was a player, and he was beyond disappointed. He was mad as hell. He had set up and handled with skill the entire complex negotiation, and now along came the boss, who was not a trained negotiator of any sort, and he would probably lose the deal.

Predictably, the boss's presentation was a joke and a disaster. He didn't know Jerome's system, and he ignored the one briefing he had allowed Jerome to give him. His presentation of features and benefits was beside the point and of no interest to the Lancelot people. It reinforced none of the vision Jerome had spent months building. In fact, it was so off-base and centered in Bonita's world that it made the other side, the Lancelot people, feel like dolts.

You know what happened. One of the Lancelot team called Jerome's boss the very next day and announced that Lancelot had no further interest in Bonita or its proposal. It was over.

Now, what would almost all negotiators in Jerome's situation do? They would accept this "no" as final, bad-mouth their boss, and perhaps look for a new position (who could blame them for this?). What did Jerome do? He took the "no" from Lancelot as he took every "no": It was a decision to be changed. He kept negotiating. He controlled his emotions and stayed in the system. The other side may have been disgusted with his boss, with good reason, but he knew this deal wasn't dead, because he knew that while he had spent a great deal of time and energy and money, the total price was still within budget. He had some of each left to "spend." Just as important, he knew that the other company's budget was *also* very high by this time. He knew their issues intimately. He had built mountains of vivid vision in their world. He understood that the greater their vision of the problem, the greater their budget would be. They, too, had incentives to get the negotiation back on track. So Jerome made the calls, wrote the letters, mended the fences—and soon closed the deal.

The moral of this story is that if you monitor and manage your budget, if you monitor and perhaps even build their budget, and if you serve your mission and purpose, you're okay regardless of what even an untrained, uninformed boss does.

Now one final story about a budget that got so out-of-control the end result is almost incomprehensible. This is the FBI's infamous Virtual Case File project from the early 2000s. What an unfathomable fiasco—as bad as any in the recent history of the federal bureaucracy, and that's saying something! In order to provide the agents in the field with the latest and best computer applications, the FBI contracted with Science Applications International Corp. (SAIC) to build a complex system. Problems followed. Delays followed. Requests for more money followed. Again and again, the FBI wrote the check. Why? The greater the investment in budget—time, energy, money, and emotion—the greater the commitment to *stay the course* and *salvage something.* In the end, the FBI had invested over $100 million and did not have a single piece of working software to show for it. Not one. It was the most widely publicized software failure in the industry's short history. When the budget gets out of control, look only to yourself. This was terrible budgeting, terrible decisions, and terrible mission and purpose—total failure.

Three-Minute Checklist

- Have you carefully considered your budget for time, for energy, for money, and for emotions? Or are you just out there chasing time, spending money, and investing emotion? *Control* your budgets.
- Do you know their budgets? *Build* their budgets.

12

Perfect Preparation

The Ultimate Advantage in Any Negotiation

f I were reading this book for the first time, I'd be asking one question right now: How do I bring together the principles of the "No" system? The answer is Checklists and Logs. These two tools provide you with the ultimate game plan, if you will, with a solid plan of execution that will always keep you safe and in reasonable control of the negotiation: all in all, maximum opportunity with the minimum possible risk. That's a good deal. They are indispensable in helping you assess your work, pinpointing weaknesses to work on and strengths to build on.

You prepare a Checklist before any meeting in any negotiation, any significant phone call, and any significant *e-mail.* After that meeting, phone call, or exchange of e-mails, you record all the significant information in your Log. You then use that Log to prepare for the next Checklist before the next encounter.

The basic Checklist for any negotiation includes:

- Your mission and purpose for the negotiation
- Your agenda items for the specific meeting
- Your behavior goals
- Your activity goals

• Any critical research that needs to be done

The Log prepared after any negotiation includes:

• Statement of the problem from the other side's point of view
• Estimate of the other side's budget (time, energy, money, and emotion)
• Identification of the decision-makers and assessment of when their decision will be reached
• Negotiation summary

> **With the Checklist *before* the meeting, you**
> **set up the structure with which to build vision**
> **on the other side. With the Log *after***
> **the meeting, you gather together the vision**
> **that exists at the end of the meeting,**
> **lay everything out, look at it, and find ways**
> **to build more vision and move ahead.**

Keeping Checklists and Logs will considerably speed up your ability to apply what you've learned in this book. Once their preparation is mastered, they will become an invaluable *lifelong* habit, believe me. My longest-term clients use them as diligently today as they did twenty years ago. So do I.

I suggest you begin developing this skill and habit a little bit at a time: a meeting here, a meeting there, a significant phone call or e-mail. Before the first modest test-drive meeting, sit down and prepare your Checklist. Of course, before you can do this you will have to think carefully about the principles that drive the elements of the Checklist, starting with mission and purpose. Select one or two behavior goals to focus on (asking good interrogative-led questions, nurturing, and giving permission to say no would be good starters). Prepare your agenda and do any research you need to do, and you'll be on your way.

In that first meeting, have the agenda and the behavioral goals noted unobtrusively among the papers in front of you. (You'll have your notepad in front of you, and you'll use it carefully.) As soon as possible after the handshakes at the end of the meeting, use your notes to prepare your Log. This will give you the opportunity to pull together what happened at the meeting and where the negotiation stands in terms of moving forward.

I will bet you right now that this before-and-after exercise will be useful from the first try. It helps you organize, helps you think in a structured, disciplined manner, and helps you control your behavior. It's that simple. In fact, Checklist and Log *make* you do all this.

Now you're ready for a second foot in the water—another meeting for which you prepare another Checklist and follow up with the Log. Then a third, then a fourth. You'll be amazed by how you acquire a feeling for their value. This process could go quickly or it could go slowly, but it will go surely. When you feel reasonably comfortable with these tools, you will be ready to implement them—and the whole "No" system—in one specific negotiation. I'd choose a pretty straightforward one, a situation that you feel comfortable with already, maybe not the most important negotiation in your shop right now. I'd say to myself, "Okay, here we go with the 'No' system. Let's just see what happens."

You prepare the Checklist going into the first meeting and the Log after the meeting. Before the second meeting of the same negotiation, you prepare the second Checklist, taking into account information in your Log of the first meeting. The Log of the second meeting helps you prepare the Checklist for the third meeting. And so it goes, meeting by meeting (maybe phone call by phone call, maybe e-mail by e-mail). The negotiation then wraps up, one way or another. You think about how things went, then you pick another negotiation to do Camp-style, and you start again. First you crawl, then you walk, and then . . . you *dance*. This is when it really gets fun.

Below are two sample Checklists and Logs from an in-house salary negotiation. Clyde Jones is seeking a substantial raise from the two founders of Bonanza, Inc., Tom Norton and Alexandra Smith, both of whom hit it big with a large software company before striking out on their own. Their new company has survived the recent hard times in the industry while modestly expanding from a handful of employees to about thirty. It has increasing revenues but had large start-up costs. There's no bureaucracy (for example, no personnel department to deal with compensation issues). Every employee is just one level from the top. The term "co-entrepreneur" is often used in company memos. Clyde has been working very long hours in business development and product testing. His salary is $40,000, not high at all given the cost of living in the region and the demands of the work. There are IPO rumors, however, and a general feeling that while salaries are low now, everyone will be rewarded when Bonanza strikes pay dirt.

CHECKLIST #1

Mission and Purpose (FOR THIS NEGOTIATION)

To provide Tom Norton and the company the very best business development team that will assure success well into the future.

Agenda

Problems (anything you see that may hinder your negotiation)

I don't know Tom's vision for compensation or his plan for the future for us as a company.

Your Baggage (any past event or opinion that you emotionally carry into the negotiation that could affect and hinder your decision-making)

None

Their Baggage (your assumptions about the company's world, opinions, and assumptions)

Prior to IPOs, many companies try to hold down their expenses and especially their salary obligations.

What You Want (most often, the rejection or acceptance of proposals or solutions that you bring forward)

For Tom to share his vision of the future and how the leadership of the company sees salary increases and performance bonuses being rewarded.

What Happens Next (your negotiated future actions)

Schedule second private meeting with Tom to discuss his findings and thoughts.

Behavior Goals (what to say and how to say it)

Early in the meeting, make these points:

> I wanted to meet with you to discuss compensation and our future. The problem is that I have not communicated my concerns of my salary and bonus opportunities with you and I don't know your vision for the future.

> What does it look like to you? Where are we headed? How should I approach this? What would be the best way?

> When will the company be in a position to make increases? Who else will make that decision besides you?

Activity Goals (WHAT YOU DO WITH TIME—TAKE NOTES, RUN A PROJECTOR, PREPARE A CHECKLIST, 3+, ETC.)

Take good notes

3+

Critical Research

Contact headhunter and check want ads to determine my market value.

LOG #1

The Problem (anything I saw in the meeting that may hinder the negotiation)

He wants to build something.

He wants people who wanted to be part of something different.

He doesn't believe people work as hard or as creatively if they're treated like replaceable employees. That's why he uses the term "co-entrepreneurs."

He'd like to make millionaires out of everyone who sticks with the company.

He must keep cost down for the IPO.

Alexandra is the lead in the IPO; she will help with this.

He will talk with Alexandra and get back to me.

Right now I need to focus on getting the next version of Webspeed! out there.

"Wednesday morning at ten we get together on this, then?"

"Next Wednesday? [3+] Good. I will draw up something for next Wednesday. Wednesday at ten it is."

Budget on the Other Side

Time

Tom spent thirty minutes with me.

Energy

Same as time. But Tom will be spending additional energy with Alexandra when he confronts her about the situation.

Money

None at this time

Emotion

Tom showed a little emotion when he admitted that he needed to make himself clear on the differences between a co-entrepreneur and an employee.

Decision (BY WHOM, WHEN, AND HOW THE DECISION WILL BE MADE)

Tom and Alexandra will make this decision.

Negotiation Summary

We will meet next Wednesday to discuss this. Tom has a vision of building a company and taking everyone loyal to him with him. Alexandra is a key player in the IPO—information I obtained that will be important in the meeting on Wednesday.

CHECKLIST #2

Mission and Purpose (FOR THIS NEGOTIATION)

To provide Tom Norton the opportunity to visualize the benefits he and the company receive from my expertise and discipline in the software arena.

Agenda

Problems

The company must hold down cost prior to an IPO. Raises are out of the question until the IPO is complete.

Can I ride the ride until after the IPO? How much risk am I willing to take? How much stress can I endure at home?

I lack Tom and Alexandra's vision for how valuable they see me to the company's success and what my compensation package will look like after the IPO.

My Baggage

None

Their Baggage

None

What I Want

Tom and Alexandra to reject or embrace a solution to my dilemma of pay and bonus.

What Happens Next

To be determined

Behavior Goals (what to say and how to say it)

Early in the meeting, make these points:

Tom and Alexandra, I really appreciate your taking the time to sit down with me. Tell me if I am wrong, but the problem I see—and I am anxious for your thoughts—is that it is important that the company keep costs down as you build the case to go public.

How do we overcome that with my compensation?

What can we do?

How could we beat that with stock?

The other problem is that my research shows that I am $20,000 to $50,000 below compensation levels and have been for the last two years.

What can be done?

What are your thoughts?

Activity Goals (WHAT YOU DO WITH TIME—TAKE NOTES, RUN A PROJECTOR, PREPARE A CHECKLIST, 3+, ETC.)

Nurture

3+

Speak softly and slowly

Take good notes

Critical Research

Talk with an accountant and get the best opinion on the value of the company.

Search the Web for jobs throughout the country. Pay close attention to the salary for similar positions.

LOG #2

The Problem

Tom wants me to hold on for six months.

Tom proposes a loan from him until the IPO is over.

Right after the IPO, I'll get a performance bonus of $20,000 and then an immediate raise of $20,000 annual. Tom wants to know how that sounds to me.

Stock options? Tom wants to think this over and then get back to me. We'll meet in a month or two. In the meantime, he will draw up an agreement.

Budget on the Other Side

Time
Thirty minutes with me

Energy
Thirty minutes with me, plus the energy he spent when speaking with Alexandra

Money
$20,000 bonus and $20,000 increase in salary

Emotion
Tom became emotional when he said that his hands were tied. He appeared upset that he could not be more effective today.

Decision
Still Tom and Alexandra

Negotiation Summary
I am pleased that Tom made me an offer of solution. I look forward to finding out what the IPO terms and conditions will be.

There's no doubt that you will benefit a great deal by incorporating in your negotiations even the most basic understanding of the principles of the "No" system. Exponentially more beneficial will be working with Checklists and Logs to tie everything together and help you evaluate your progress. I urge you—I beg you—to give Checklist and Log a test drive. I realize it's easy for me to make this request, and it's even easy for you to decide to do it, but in today's hectic world, well, it may be difficult to knuckle down. As a coach *in absentia* I don't enjoy any powers of oversight here, much less enforcement, but the exercise will pay enormous dividends for everyone who gives it a try.

I wrote in the Introduction that my system is pretty easy to understand in its basics but requires discipline and patience and practice. I'll stand by that statement here in the Conclusion. Learning doesn't come automatically—not at all—and you may face some challenges implementing some of the more counterintuitive principles of my system—"no," for example. How long before you completely own this system? Without hands-on training, that's probably asking too much. Full and complete implementation of the system in this book requires a great deal of discipline, as I've stated time and again, and it's difficult to maintain such discipline in any endeavor when working alone. (This is one reason almost no top athletes train alone.)

How long before you feel *a lot more comfortable* than you may feel right now, and without hands-on coaching? How long before you feel a lot more comfortable on the dance floor that is negotiation? How long before Checklist and Log and all the principles they incorporate flow almost organically through your work? As I've said, any complex new activity requires at least 800 hours before most of us will master the discipline, according to one study. That's twenty 40-hour weeks—five months. Sounds about right, but who knows? I've had new clients pick up the "No" system so quickly it was scary—a couple of months. Others have taken much longer but achieved the same level of success in the end. (And all those champions are still working hard, because no one works harder than the best to get even better. This is why Tiger Woods has rebuilt his golf swing not once but twice as a professional. Already incredibly good as a teenager, he believed he could get even better—and he did. Nobel Prize winners don't rest on their laurels. Bill Gates and Steve Jobs and Warren Buffett don't sit back and waste time counting their money. They seek new challenges.)

So maybe it will take two months before you feel pretty comfortable, maybe six months, maybe longer. Who's counting? All I know is this: Every day you'll become more adept with the system and more confident that it works and more knowledgeable about how and why it works. Every day you'll be a better negotiator than you were the day before, and one day, *for the first time in your business life,* you'll start to achieve at a level approaching your potential.

I guarantee it.

If You Want More

If you have read straight through this book without taking any of the test drives and without executing any Checklists and Logs, you're probably not ready for the material that will follow. But that's not to discourage you from reading it all the same. If you have put some of the negotiating tools of the "No" system into practice, however, you might be ready for more advanced training through the challenge of some of the more rigorous activities below.

- Every morning, write down the Behavior Goals you are working on for that day. At the end of each day, evaluate your performance.
- Every morning, write down the Activity Goals you are working on for that day. At the end of each day, evaluate your performance.
- Do outside reading. (If you contact us, we can provide you with a reading list of 187 volumes of great thinkers in many different disciplines that will help enhance and support your efforts.)
- Join our self-directed lessons program or one of our advanced training and coaching programs, up to and including becoming a coach.
- Keep a Personal Journal of Observations and Reflections. (Journal keeping is a lost art but a very valuable tool in personal development. By making a note of your failures and your successes, you will enhance your thought processes as you grow in your negotiations.)

- Be disciplined about your Checklists and Logs. Be organized about your Checklists and Logs. Simply put a binder together with Checklist and then Log, Checklist and then Log. (When you can save everything on your computer, this may not seem necessary, but you're just going to have to trust me on this one.)

You still want more?

- Go to our website; we'll challenge you.
www.startwithno.com

Acknowledgments

A small group of people made large contributions to this book. John Mahaney, my editor at Crown Business, pushed and pulled this book through the changes required in order to get us to *No*. Thank you, John; this book wouldn't be here without you. Nor would it be here without Mike Bryan, who helped the book get going, and Patty Bryan, who delivered outstanding support pushing me to think outside my comfort zone. Thank you must go to my two sons, Todd and Jim Camp, Head Coaches in our organization who contributed many of the incredible stories in this book from their own coaching experiences.

Many thanks to John Thornton and Joe Spieler, my agents, for their stability and guidance.

Bob Jordan also deserves much credit because Bob is the guy who talked me into going public in print with my system in the first place.

Ahead of time, so to speak, I want to thank Cathy Lewis for her great help with publicity and promotion. She's the best. And thanks up front to the Crown folks who will work with Cathy.

I also want to thank our many corporate clients and individuals who have given us the opportunity to grow into our leadership position in the most important human-performance event: negotiation. Without them, these ideas would only be theory instead of the new standard in the field.

Finally, I want to thank Patty, my wife, soul mate, and the love of my life, for the support, patience, tolerance, and grounding without which none of this would be happening.

Index

About the Author

Jim Camp has coached people through thousands of negotiations at more than 500 companies and organizations (both large and small) in a broad range of industries, including Texas Instruments, Intel, Applied Materials, Merrill Lynch, IBM, Cisco Systems, KLA-Tencor, Prudential Insurance, Nationwide Insurance, and the Pentagon. His first book, *Start with No,* is required reading for MBA candidates at several universities, including New York University and the University of Florida. He has lectured widely in the United States as well as in Russia, Romania, Hungary, England, Germany, Singapore, Japan, and China. He is the inventor of his proprietary Coach2100 Project Management System for Negotiation and president and CEO of Coach2100, Inc. To review Jim's coaching programs for individuals and industry, visit www.startwithno.com.